# TEACHING ENGLISH

*A HANDBOOK FOR PRECEPTORS*

# TEACHING ENGLISH
## *A HANDBOOK FOR PRECEPTORS*

*By*

**Dr. R. Ramar**
*Principal*
*PSR College of Education*
*Sivakasi (Tamilnadu)*
*(INDIA)*

*&*

**R.T. Sivaram**
*Post Graduate English Teacher*
*Nadar Higher Secondary School*
*Thalavaipuram (Tamilnadu)*
*(INDIA)*

DPH

**DISCOVERY PUBLISHING HOUSE PVT. LTD.**
**NEW DELHI-110 002**

*Published by:*

**Namit Wasan**

**DISCOVERY PUBLISHING HOUSE PVT. LTD.**

4383/4B, Ansari Road, Darya Ganj

New Delhi-110 002 (India)

*Phone* : +91-11-23279245, 43596064-65

*Fax* : +91-11-23253475

*E-mail* : discoverypublishinghouse@gmail.com
namitwasan9@gmail.com
sales@discoverypublishinggroup.com

*web* : www.discoverypublishinggroup.com

*First Edition:* **2016**

**ISBN: 978-93-5056-774-6**

**Teaching English: *A Handbook for Preceptors***



*Printed at:*
Infinity Imaging Systems
Delhi

# Preface

English is a foreign language and it is learnt as a second language all over India. There are many basic concepts underlying the teaching and learning of English in India. We have made an earnest attempt in this book to present all the vital aspects of teaching English as a foreign as well as a second language in India in the simplest possible manner. This book has been designed as a handbook for the present as well as future preceptors.

This book aims at offering practical help to the teachers to develop an adequate insight into the problems encountered in teaching English as a foreign/second language and also provides concrete solutions to overcome the problems. This book will be of immense use to the teachers as well as student teachers who are keen on learning such various methods and techniques that are effective in teaching and learning of English language.

This book adequately covers the English syllabus prescribed for the B.Ed., course in most of the Indian universities. This book dwells upon almost all aspects of teaching English like the nature and scope of English language, aims and objectives of teaching English as a second language, problems in teaching and learning of English, principles of English language teaching, teaching skills, resources in teaching English, approaches and methods of teaching English, tools of evaluation and educational statistics. In addition, last four units deal with development of listening, speaking reading and writing skills at lower as well as higher level.

Every possible effort has been taken to keep the description clear, simple and brief. As this book is free from linguistic jargon, it will be of great use to teachers in service, student teachers and teacher educators. They will find it easy to understand the concepts and to retain them in memory for their future use. We are very much indebted to all the eminent writers whose books and research papers have had indelible impact on our learning of the subject.

We sincerely believe that this book will receive wide acclaim from student teachers, teacher educators and practising preceptors across the country because in its content and design as well as in its approach and presentation, it is exactly the kind of text book much needed by the students of various universities in India.

**–Authors**

# Contents

# 1 Nature, Need and Objectives of Teaching English

## THE STATUS OF ENGLISH IN INDIA

### Status of English Before Independence

English occupied an important place in India before independence. It was the official language of the administration. It was the medium of instruction and a subject of study in schools and colleges. Knowledge of English was a symbol of status. It was the link language in different countries of the world.

### Status of English Now

Now English is the associate official language in India. It occupies an important place in court, commerce and industry. It is a link and library language in India. English is window of the world. It is widely used for interstate and centre state communication between governments. India is a land of multiple languages. So, English is still a Lingua Franca. English is still the favoured medium of instruction at higher level.

### The Rationale for Learning English

The fundamental reasons and logical bases for learning English are as follows:

1. English plays a vital role in getting placement, career growth and development. It is considered a valid passport for national employments.
2. English lays the royal road to a variety of sources of information and knowledge. We cannot develop an

accurate insight into the developments of science and technology without an adequate knowledge of English.

3. English is essential to learn more about people, the people of other nations, their way of life, their culture etc.
4. English is an international language. Knowledge of English is essential for social interaction and business transaction with the people and firms of other countries.
5. English is the link language within India also. We need English for personal interaction, social transaction and for official communication with people and firms of other states.
6. English is a literary language. It is reputed to have a rich literature with a wide variety.
7. It is a library language. All the inventions, scientific findings and technological innovations are first published in English. So, it enables us to keep ourselves abreast of the latest.
8. English is a window through which we can see the world. It promotes international understanding. It binds and brings people together.
9. English enables us to use the leisure time properly. While reading for pleasure also, our knowledge is enriched.
10. English plays a vital role in our social and cultural life. It plays an instrumental role in national and international politics.

## AIMS OFTEACHING ENGLISH AT PRIMARY, SECONDARY AND HIGHER SECONDARY LEVELS

*Aims of teaching English at primary level:*

The following are the aims of teaching English at primary level:

- To learn alphabets.
- To gain ability to read.
- To have sufficient vocabulary.
- To understand spoken English.
- To make small and simple statement.
- To answer simple conversational questions.
- To write English neatly.

- To identify things by their name.
- To learn small letters.
- To practise cursive writing.

*Aims of teaching English at secondary level:*

The aims of teaching English at secondary level are:

- To understand spoken English.
- To speak simple sentences.
- To read passages in English without mistake.
- To spell words with correct pronunciation.
- To make simple sentences using the content and structural words.
- To respond to simple conversation.
- To write application letters.
- To read English newspaper.

*Aims of teaching English at higher secondary level:*

The aims of teaching English at higher secondary level include:

- To be able to speak English fluently and accurately.
- To read English newspaper regularly and rapidly.
- To develop the ability to understand native speakers and to respond to them.
- To make narratives and to take notes.
- To read English novels and understand them.
- To express ideas coherently in the gathering.
- To use reference materials such as dictionaries, thesaurus and encyclopaedia.
- To acquire vocabulary of about 3000 words.
- To enjoy and sing poems.
- To understand message and advertisements.
- To perform English plays in the school functions.
- To appreciate the beauty of the poems.
- To punctuate correctly while writing.
- To know the functional use of grammar.
- To apply for a job looking at the advertisements in the newspaper.
- To summarise and comprehend the English passage.

- To write all types of letters
- To write at a reasonable speed
- To have knowledge on the uses of stresses and intonation

## OBJECTIVES OFTEACHING ENGLISH AS A SECOND LANGUAGE

Objectives of teaching English as a second language include Cultural, literary, utilitarian, linguistic and integrative aims.

### Cultural Aims

English brings people of diverse cultures close to one another. It promotes inter-cultural understanding. It facilitates modernisation of society. It dispels our ignorance and superstitions. Language is a verbal behaviour and it is beliefs of society. Language is the embodiment of culture.

### Literary Aims

It was in English classroom that Indian literary renaissance was born. English literature is rich with works of higher order in the field of poetry, drama, fiction, art etc. Wide variety is the special feature of English literature. All subjects are studied in English at advanced level. It has the most original publications. All research findings are documented in English.

### Utilitarian Aims

English is the most widely spoken language in the world. It is the mother tongue of more than 300 million people. Another 200 million people use it as second language. English is used throughout the globe. Some Indian states and territories i.e Nagaland, Mizoram, Arunachal Pradesh, Meghalaya and Sikkim have adopted English as their official language. M.C. Chagla, the Chief Justice of Bombay high court once ruled that English was an Indian language and the Supreme Court upheld this judgement. Sahitaya Academy recognises English as one of the Indian languages. Because of its great popularity and worldwide distribution it is the medium of international communication. English is used in trade, commerce and diplomatic relation with other countries. Hence learning English is a must for everyone.

### Linguistic Aims

Linguistics is defined as a scientific study of language. It aims to seek scientific understanding of language. Linguistics aims at classifying the four aspects of language (i.e) pronunciation, vocabulary grammar and relationship between speaker and listener. So the linguistic aim of teaching English is to make English language clearly understandable to everyone.

### Integrative Aims

The Indian Education Commission (1964-66) has recommended the continuance of English in the interest of national integration and for highest academic work. English is a subject of study upto graduation level. English helped the growth of nationalism which ultimately freed the country from British yoke. Now also it is the national link language for interstate and centre state correspondences. It helps us to understand the world situations and affairs. It is a must for students going abroad for higher education. So the integrative aim of teaching English is to promote national integration and a sense of belongingness to the international community.

## CONTRIBUTION OF LINGUISTICS AND PSYCHOLOGY TO TEACHING OF ENGLISH

Linguistics and psychology have made significant contributions to teaching of English as a second language. They are discussed below.

### Contribution of Linguistics

Linguistics has given us the study of mechanism of language. It tells us the way a language works. It deals with the forms and manifestations of language. It classifies the four aspects of language i.e. Pronunciation, vocabulary, grammar, and relationship between speakers. It has provided terminology which can be used by lexicographers, translators, speech therapists, language teachers etc. Linguistics' contributions to teaching are as follows.

1. A disinterested enquiry into the nature of human language.
2. The methods of teaching a language.

**Contribution of Psychology to Teaching of English**

Psychology is the study of human behaviour. Several psychological principles are involved in teaching and learning of English as a second language. It has made three contributions to learning and teaching of English. They are:

1. Learning theory
2. Experimental research on teaching and learning of English
3. Laws of learning

**Psychological Principles**

The following principles are very important from educational as well as instructional point of view.

**1. Individual differences**

Language learning takes place at different rates for different persons. So language should be taught to cater to individual differences.

**2. Learning readiness**

Mental and physical readiness is essential for learning a language. So the teacher must make it sure that students are mentally ready for learning the concept or language.

**3. Memory span**

Teacher must take into consideration the memory span of the students. He must use simple and short sentences, so that the students can retain them. Constant practice and drill can enhance retention.

**4. Motivation**

High motivation enhances learning whereas low motivation results in poor learning. The teacher must motivate the students by highlighting the importance, relevance and utility of English knowledge.

**5. Total experience**

Total experience leads to better learning. So the teacher should provide total experience in the language classroom. Teacher should create ample opportunity for listening, speaking, reading and writing.

**6. Learning by imitation**

Children learn by observation and imitation. So the teacher should serve as a good model for the students to learn the language skills.

**7. Attention and awareness**

Attention lays the foundation for learning. Degree of attention decides the level of performance. So teachers should ensure that students pay attention to their expression, context and association.

**8. Immediate reinforcement**

Reinforced behaviour tends to strengthen. So teachers must let the students know whether their responses are correct or not immediately. This will help the learners develop correct language habits.

**9. Law of exercise**

Law of exercise emphasises practice. Practice enhances learning. Practice gives perfection. So most of the learning time must be used for practice.

**10. Positive attitude and interest**

Positive attitude enhances interest in learning. Negative attitude retards learning. So teacher must develop positive attitude among students towards learning English. Positive attitude promotes interest and in turn interest increases effective learning;

**11. Meaningful verbal learning**

Meaningful materials promote proper understanding and better learning. Nonsense syllables retard learning. So language should be taught in meaningful situations.

**12. Willingness and cooperation**

One's own willingness and cooperation ensure better learning. Willingness leads to cooperation and greater participation in learning activities.

**13. Facilitation and interferences**

Similarities between languages will facilitate learning and dissimilarities will be an interference. English and Indian languages don't have similarities between them. English teachers should teach English by explaining the contrastive elements of English and their mother tongue.

**14. Learner centred teaching**

Participatory learning is more effective. Learner centred teaching is more effective than teacher centred teaching. In learner centred approach, the learners are more accountable for their learning.

**15. Teaching the communication skills**

Listening, speaking, reading and writing, are the major skills in English. Teaching of communication skills includes:

1. Oral communications skills
2. Active listening skills
3. Reading skills
4. Writing skills
5. Composition skills
6. Speaking skills
7. Pronunciation skills
8. Dictionary skills

**Teaching of Communicative Skills**

As English is a skill subject, the teacher should employ the following steps in skill instruction.

1. Analyse the skill to be taught
2. Assess the entering behaviour of the student.
3. Provide training in component skills.
4. Describe and demonstrate sub-skills though instructional sequences.
5. Provide contiguity, practice and feedback to the students.
6. Make the students become autonomous in the skill.

This method of instruction is now known as the skill based teaching in language.

## LISTENING SKILLS

Listening means paying attention to what is said, read, announced, spoken or played.

It is the beginning of the learning process. Without listening one cannot understand or speak.

It includes three components i.e., hearing, listening and interpreting.

**Importance of Listening**

Listening is the base for understanding. Listening leads to speaking. So, efficient, active and attentive listening must be taught at all grade levels. According to Smith, there are four kinds of listening such as attentive, appreciative, analytical and marginal listening.

**Types of Listening**

There are two types of listening. They are:

1. Casual Listening
2. Focused Listening

**(i) Casual listening**

Casual listening means listening without much attention. It is listening while doing some work or talking with others. Listening without any specific purpose is called casual listening.

**(ii) Focused listening**

Focused listening is listening with attention and concentration. It is a purposeful listening. Listening seriously to news bulletin or important announcement is a good example for focused listening. Focused listening is required in teaching learning process.

**Techniques of Listening**

There are some techniques to develop listening skill. They are:

*(i)* developing listening through dialogue.
*(ii)* developing listening through cassette recorder.
*(iii)* developing listening through guessing.

**(i) Developing listening through dialogue:**

Listening skills can be developed through dialogue. It includes the following steps:

Introduction of the topic to provide prior knowledge.

1. Asking lead questions to draw their attention to main points.
2. First reading by the teacher to give practice.

3. Asking questions to extract answers related to main points.
4. Second reading by the teacher to provide more practice.
5. Asking questions to check comprehension.
6. Third reading by the teacher for the students to follow.
7. Providing drill and practice to strengthen listening skills.

**(ii) Developing listening through cassette recorder**

Cassettes provide a variety of voices. It makes the class lively. We can record whatever we want to listen. We can listen to whenever we want to listen to. We can play again and again till we understand. It encourages intensive reading. It is very useful for providing practice.

**(iii) Developing listening through guessing**

Making students guess what they are going to hear next is an important technique of developing listening skills. It makes the class active and involved. Students will be always in anticipation or expectation. It plays a key role in listening to narration of stories or incidents.

## SPEAKING SKILLS

Speaking means expressing one's wish or opinion to somebody orally. Teaching spoken English plays a key role in career growth and development of a person.

Teaching spoken English is important because:

1. Spelling offers no clue to pronunciation.
2. Twenty six letters do the work for forty four sounds.
3. The same letter stands for different sounds.
4. The same sound is represented by different letters.
5. Silent letters do not work.

*Teaching pronunciation:* Pronunciation refers to the way a word is pronounced. It refers to the way sound is made to represent a word. Students who learn English as a second language experience considerable difficulty in pronunciation. So teaching pronunciation becomes necessary. The guidelines given below may be followed in teaching pronunciation.

1. Pupils have to be given copious practice in listening and reproducing speech sounds.

2. We must cultivate a phonetic consciousness in our pupils.
3. We have to prevent vernacular habits of utterance in our pupil's speech.
4. The ordinary English speed of five syllables per second may be tried.
5. Speech comes before reading and the latter will be introduced only after pupils know how to pronounce the new learning items.
6. The teacher's spoken English has to be a model worthy of pupils imitation and emulation.
7. The teacher must give phonic drill in respect of sounds causing difficulty.
8. Exercises like tongue –twisters can be given.
9. The teacher should realise the importance of other aspects of spoken English like stress, intonation, interjection, facial expression and gestures.

**Major Pronunciation Problems**

Pronunciation poses considerable problems to such students who learn English as a second language. The following are the major pronunciation problems.

1. Students use their mother tongue while learning pronunciation.
2. They have no familiarity with vowel sounds.
3. They have no idea about cluster of sounds, stress and intonation.
4. They have major difficulty in orthography.

**Measures to Overcome Pronunciation Problems**

The following measures should be taken to enable the students to overcome their pronunciation problems.

1. Known sounds should be taught first to avoid confusion in pronunciation.
2. Drill and practice should be provided frequently.
3. When a new sound is introduced, teacher should use a number of words with same sound and same syllable.

**Grading of Speaking Activities**

Activities must be graded according to age groups and the level of mastery attained by the students. The most controlled kinds of drills are the imitation drills, recitation of rhyme and jingle. These are suitable for beginners. The free use kind of language drills are debate, story telling, conversation etc. These are suitable for advanced pupils.

### Teaching Stress, Rhyme and Intonation

Stress refers to the extra force used when making a particular sound. Rhyme refers to the word having same sound or ending with same sound as another word. Intonation is the rise and fall of the voice in speaking. Individual sounds can be taught easily. It is difficult to teach stress and intonation. Teachers can use cassettes. They may arrange for listening to radio broadcasts. Imitation drills can be provided. Intonation patterns can be visualised with the help of symbols.

## READING SKILLS

Reading means articulating the language symbols and understanding meaning. Reading is the major objective of the English course in schools. Reading aloud helps pronunciation. It is a source of pleasure and profit. The abilities involved in reading are

1. Ability to recognise the symbols.
2. Comprehension ability.

Reading involves sight, sound and sense i.e. recognising the symbol, articulating sound and understanding meaning.

### Two Kinds of Reading

There are two kinds of reading. They are:

1. oral reading; and
2. silent reading.

### Stages in Teaching Reading

Teaching reading includes three stages. They are:

*(i)* Preparatory stage
*(ii)* Oral reading stage
*(iii)* Silent reading stage

#### (i) Preparatory stage

During this stage no reading is done. Teacher provides speech training and oral drill.

**(ii) Oral reading stage**

Oral reading is reading aloud. Words and sentences to be read are drilled orally first. Teacher provides model reading. Then pupils read from the blackboard. After that, they read from their books. This is the procedure for early reading lessons. Later blackboard reading may be given up.

**(iii) Silent reading stage**

Silent reading is reading without making sound. It is the most important reading. After initial stage, it should be introduced. First, training in small paragraphs is given. The unit gradually lengthens and full scale silent reading is introduced.

**Methods of Teaching Reading**

There are two major methods of teaching oral reading. They are:

(a) Letter methods
(b) Non letter methods

**(a) Letter Methods**

Letter methods include:

1. The alphabet method;
2. The phonic method; and
3. The phonetic method.

**1. The alphabet method**

Letters are taught first in conventional order (a to z).Then pupils progressively begin to read words, phrases, sentences and longer units. Here the unit of teaching is letter.

**2. The phonic method**

Here basic speech sound is taught first. Word is broken into basic sounds. Students learn different sounds first. They learn alphabets later. This method is used in U.K.

**3. The phonetic method**

Here the 44 sounds of 26 letters are taught first. Teacher explains how different organs of speech produce sound. This is the most scientific of the letter methods. Correct pronunciation is instilled in pupils from the beginning.

**(b) Non letter method**

Non letter method includes:

1. The word method
2. The phrase method
3. The sentence method
4. The story method
5. Practical method

**The Word Method**

Here word is taught as a single and indivisible unit. Then only it is analysed into its component letters. The unit of teaching is word. Wren calls it the one and only rational method. It is called look and say method.

**The Phrase Method**

Here the unit of teaching is phrase. Students learn phrase first and then alphabets. Readers always recognise a group of words at each fixation of eyes. So, phrase method is emphasised.

**The Sentence Method**

Here sentence is the unit of teaching. Sentence is the unit of speech. So it is a logical method. Analysis into words and letters comes next. This method affords training in pronunciation. It enhances comprehension and fluency in reading.

**The Story Method**

This method has all the advantages of the sentence method. Teacher narrates the story in simple sentences. Pupils narrate after him. This is followed by oral drill of sentences. Then these sentences are written on the blackboard. Teacher reads and the pupils read after him. Finally, reading from the text and analysis into words and letters take place.

**Practical Method**

It is a combination of sentence method with other methods. We can combine each one of the various methods suitably. After reading sentences, there is analysis into words and letters.

### Intensive Reading and Extensive Reading

A detailed study of the prescribed reader or textbook is called intensive reading. It deals with a study of new structures and new vocabulary items. Here the students make attempt to master the language skills.

Extensive reading refers to reading longer texts like novels, stories etc. This is done for pleasure. Skipping as well as skimming is allowed. It reinforces the already learnt structures and vocabulary. It increases speed in silent reading. It increases love for extra reading.

### General Principles of Teaching Reading

The following are the general principles of teaching reading:

1. Time of starting
2. Choice of reader
3. Speech before reading
4. Training in both oral and silent reading
5. Using a psychological method
6. Playway
7. Teacher as model reader
8. Procedural reader
9. Insisting correct reading habits from the beginning
10. Reading with comprehension

## WRITING SKILL

Writing is expressing ideas, thoughts etc in words. It is one of the expressive skills to be developed in language learning. Writing provides reinforcement for reading and learning. It provides a change of activity. According to Bacon writing makes an exact man.

### Mechanics of Writing

Mechanics refers to how a composition is arranged on paper. Letter formation, spacing of words, paragraph alignment, spelling, punctuation etc are all parts of mechanics of writing. Mechanics of writing includes right shape and size of letters and proper spacing between letters, words and lines.

1. Using capital and punctuation marks correctly
2. Speed in writing
3. Using forms and register appropriate for the subject and audience.

**Two Types of Script**

There are two types of script. They are:

1. Print script
2. Cursive script

**Print Script**

Print script refers to writing the letters separately. It is identical with the script of the text book. It is easy to write. It is suitable for beginners but it reduces speed.

**Cursive Script**

It is the running hand script. Here the letters are joined together. It enhances speed in writing. It is matured way of writing. It is adult way of writing.

**Italic Hand Writing**

Italic writing is one of the many styles of writing. This is the most widely accepted writing. It is easy to write, graceful to look at and legible to read.

## TEACHING ENGLISH AS SKILL RATHER THAN KNOWLEDGE SUBJECT

Language is often called a skill subject. It is not a knowledge subject. It is more a matter of doing than knowing. Learning a language is a matter of practice. As we learn cycling or swimming, we can learn English effectively. Teachers should have some knowledge about application of certain principles.

**Basic Principles of Teaching a Language**

Some of the basic principles of teaching a language are as follows limitation. Learning of any language is based on the principle of imitation. In fact, imitation is natural to man. So an English teacher should have a model type of pronunciation, handwriting and habits for his students to imitate.

**Practice and Drill**

Language learning is a habit formation process. Habits are formed through repetition. It needs continuous practice and drill. The quantity of learning or the mastery of language is in direct proportion to the amount of practice.

**Oral Approach**

Language is more connected with ears and tongue than with eyes. So, oral work should be given priority. If good at spoken language, the students will be good at reading and writing also. Moreover, oral work enhances memory.

**Selection and Gradation**

Selection should be done in respect of grammatical item, vocabulary and structures. Selection should be based on frequency of occurrence, availability, teachability and also learn ability.

**Motivation of Interest**

Language is learnt quickly if there is interest in learning the language. So, teachers should use different aids and techniques to create interest. Some interesting methods like activity method and play way method can be used.

**Context and Situation**

Language items such as vocabulary and structures should be used in the context of life situations and classroom situation. This will enable the learners to understand the meanings of words and usages of structures in a better way.

**Multiple Line of Approach**

Multiple line of approach includes oral work, written work and practice, translation and correlation. This will make language learning easy, interesting and useful.

**Balanced Approach**

LSRW skills should be equally emphasised. There must be a balance between oral work and written work. There must be a balance between prose and poetry, grammar and composition, etc.

**Natural Way of Learning**

LSRW skills should be developed in natural order. Listening will lead to speaking. Students good at speaking become good at reading and writing.

### General Maxims

General maxims such as easy to difficult, simple to complex, known to unknown, particulars to general, concrete to abstract should be followed in teaching English language.

## GENERAL PRINCIPLES OFTEACHING LANGUAGE

According to Robert Lado (1964) the language teaching involves the following general principles.

1. Speech before writing
2. Pattern of habits
3. Basic sentences
4. Sound system for use
5. Vocabulary control
6. Writing as representation by speech
7. Graded patterns
8. Language practice versus translation practice
9. Shaping of responses
10. Immediate reinforcement
11. Teaching for learning outcome

## LEARNING THE MOTHER TONGUE AND LEARNING A SECOND LANGUAGE

Mother tongue is the language that a child learns from mother. Mother tongue is as natural for development of mind as mother's milk is for the development of the body. Communication through mother tongue begins at the earliest stage of life. Mother tongue helps the child in all kinds of thinking and mental operations like elaborating, enquiring, reasoning, analysing, discussing, etc. Mother tongue is the basic of all works. The child learns new words, uses them in proper contexts and acquires ability to express. Acquisition of these skills is natural, gradual but unconscious.

| Learning Mother Tongue | Learning Other Tongue |
|---|---|
| It is a natural process.<br>There is no hindrance | It is an artificial process.<br>There is a hindrance in learning. |
| Our natural urges, needs and social set up play a compulsive role. | This does not occur in learning other tongue i.e. English |

*(Contd...)*

| Learning Mother Tongue | Learning Other Tongue |
|---|---|
| We are helped by family members, friends, relatives, teachers, society and everyone in learning the mother tongue. | This is not possible in the learning of other tongue i.e. english. |
| Learner has listening opportunity at home and everywhere. | This is not so in the case of English – Listening opportunity is limited |
| He has exposure to language all the time. | Here there is very limited exposure. |
| There is no break in the practice of the speech. | There is break when there is vacation or change in the environment. |

**The way the mother tongue helps in learning english:**

1. In the learning of the mother tongue the child forms habits. i.e. LSRW. The same habits are needed and developed in the learning of English language.
2. The sounds similar in both languages facilitate the learning of the new language.(i.e.) English.
3. Grammatical items common in both the languages promote easy learning.
4. In the mother tongue, the imagination of the child is developed. It is very helpful in learning of English.
5. Sitting, holding pen, writing and consulting a dictionary are taught in mother tongue. It helps in learning of English.
6. For full comprehension, mother tongue helps considerably. Use of mother tongue at early stages and teacher's translation now and then help a good deal in learning English.

**Interference of Mother Tongue in Learning of English:**

1. No two languages are alike. It is difficult to find exact equivalents. Translation may be approximate but not exact. This affects learning of English.
2. English has 26 alphabets and Tamil has 216 alphabets. All Indian languages have more letters than English. These alphabets are used to produce all the sounds. It confuses the learners.

3. Tamil is a phonetic language. English is unphonetic. So learner faces a number of problems.
4. A few consonant sounds of English are not found in other languages. This creates problems for the learners.
5. Stress, rhythm, intonation of Indian languages and English differ widely. This also causes problems for the young learners.
6. The sentence patterns of English and Indian languages are different. Interrogative sentences of English and Indian languages are also different. This confuses the learners.
7. In mother tongue, adjectives undergo a change according to number or gender. But in English it does not change. Ex: He is good. She is good mtd} ey;ytd}. mts} ey;yts}.
8. The structural words of Tamil and English are not equivalent.
9. In Tamil, students have the habit of producing same sound. In English some letters have different sounds and some sounds are made by different letters.

**Transfer of Learning from Mother Tongue**

If a child can talk freely and fluently in his mother tongue, he can speak well and easily in any language. The oral expression in English greatly depends upon the oral expression in mother tongue. Before the students are asked to relate the story in English, they must be able to relate it in mother tongue.

**Use in Pronunciation**

Clear pronunciation in English is possible only when the pupil's pronunciation in mother tongue is clear. English has a complex system of vowels and diphthongs. These are not found in Indian languages. So before giving pronunciation drill, articulation should be pointed out.

**Use in Reading**

Children who can read well in mother tongue can quickly learn reading English. Reading exercise given in mother tongue can develop pupil's reading attention, reading posture, and reading habits.

### Use in Grammar

The grammar learnt by the child in mother tongue forms the background for English grammar. This makes the work of the English teacher easy. Mother tongue can be used to explain grammar. A comparison and contrast of English and mother tongue grammatical forms will facilitate better learning.

### Use in Translations

Mother tongue plays a key role in translation. It gives the students adequate practice in expressing English using the nearest equivalent in mother tongue.

### Use in Composition

All the subject matters for written composition can be borrowed from mother tongue. Practice in the organisation of ideas can be gained through mother tongue. The topic covered in mother tongue can be attempted for English composition.

### Implications for Teaching Methods

Transfer of learning from mother tongue has far reaching implications for teaching methods.

There must be concentration on speech. Listening and speaking should precede reading and writing.

1. Learning English through translations and study of grammar should be discouraged.
2. Language activity should be associated with child's situation.
3. Classes and groups must be small, large class room will affect the pace of learning.
4. Learning process must have variety. It should not be monotonous.
5. Constant revision, drill and practice must be provided for mastery learning.

## SCOPE OFTHE B.ED ENGLISH COURSE

1. B.ed. Programme prepares the student teachers for placement at secondary and higher secondary levels. It provides the skill and knowledge required for teaching English at secondary level.

2. Career opportunities are more for English teachers in variety of fields such as law, medicine, engineering, education etc.
3. B.ed. course offers training to develop communicative skills besides offering a wide variety of methods and techniques of teaching English.
4. In B.ed. course, phonetics and spoken language are adequately covered.
5. English is a compulsory subject in schools and colleges. B.ed. course prepares teachers for placement at various levels.
6. English enables individuals to negotiate their own salaries with multinational employers.

## SUMMARY

English occupied an important place in India before independence. It was official language, medium of instruction, subject of study and a symbol of status. Now also English is the associate official language in India. It is widely used in court, commerce and industry. It is still a link and library language in India. It is used for interstate and centre state communication between governments.

The rationale for learning English includes smooth way for placement, career growth and development, royal road to a variety of sources of information and knowledge, use of English for interaction, social transaction and official/business communication transcending boundaries, link value, literary value and international understanding.

There are specific aims of teaching English for primary level, secondary level and higher secondary level, which are progressive. Objectives of teaching as a second language includes cultural aims, literary aim, utilitarian aim, linguistic aim and integrative aim. Each aim of teaching English as a second language has its own importance.

Linguistics and psychology have made significant contributions to teaching of English. Contribution of linguistics includes a disinterested enquiry into the nature of human language and the methods of teaching. Learning theories, experimental researches on teaching and learning of English and laws of learning are the important contributions made by psychology to teaching of English.

Listening is paying attention to what is said, announced or played. There are two types of listening: casual listening and focused listening. The techniques to develop listening skill include developing listening skill through dialogue, through cassette recorder and through guessing. Listening leads to speaking. So active and attentive listening must be taught at all grade levels.

Speaking means expressing one's wish or opinion to somebody orally. Spoken English plays a key role in career growth and development of a person. Students experience considerable difficulty in pronunciation. There are specific measures to overcome pronunciation problems. Speaking activities must be graded according to age groups and mastery level of students.

Reading means articulating the language symbols and understanding meaning. Reading skills include ability to recognise symbols and ability to understand. There are two kinds of reading: oral reading and silent reading. Preparatory stage, oral reading stage and silent reading stage are the stages in teaching reading. Methods of teaching reading includes letter methods and non letter methods.

Writing is expressing ideas, thoughts etc in words. Mechanics of writing includes using capital and punctuation marks correctly, speed in writing and using forms and registers appropriate for the subject and audience. Print script and cursive script are the two types of script. Italic writing is one of the many styles of writing.

English is a skill subject. Basic principles of teaching a language are imitation, practice and drill, oral approach, selection and gradation, context and situation, motivation etc. Learning a second language is different from learning mother tongue. Mother tongue facilitates transfer of learning and helps in learning of english. At the same time, mother tongue makes its own interferences in learning of english.

# 2 Problems in Teaching and Learning of English in India

The conditions under which English is taught in Indian schools differ from state to state and from one type of schools to another. English is taught under favourable conditions in public schools, Anglo-Indian schools and in some of the Matriculation schools whereas the conditions under which it is taught in most of the schools in any state for that matter are not favourable.

English has been included in the school curriculum as a second language or as a language of study for practical utility. Its study is compulsory for everyone. There are good many teachers of English in Indian schools nevertheless, the standard of the students is not up to the mark. It is rather sad to say that there is something wrong with the teaching of English in Indian schools. There are certain problems which need to be tackled tactfully. Before delving into the problems in detail let us examine the conditions under which English is taught in our country.

Prof. V.K. Gokak says, "The study of English in our schools is in a chaotic state today. Pupils are taught English for about six periods a week for six years. But it has been estimated that they hardly know 1500 words by the time they join a university. This means that they have hardly been able to learn English words at the rate of one word per period. They do not know how to use the commonest structures of English."

We cannot simply say that there is something wrong with the teaching of English in Indian school. There is something wrong with the learning of English also. In this context it is apt to recall what Michael West has said. He observes, "A language is not a subject which can be taught; it is a subject which must be learnt." We must make efforts to rectify the defects. In the word of Harold Palmer, "What has been badly assimilated must be eliminated consciously". According to V.K. Gokak, "Teaching of English is in a chaotic state today."

A glance at the present situation brings to light the sorry state affairs. Everybody is after the examination. A student doesn't bother about acquiring real knowledge of learning of the language. He makes all possible efforts to succeed in getting the diploma or the degree. What he wants most is score, not knowledge or skill. He strives hard to get high score by any means. On the other hand, the teacher is bent on enabling the students to pass in the examination. He is very particular that his pass percentage should not go down. As a result, English is not taught as it should be taught by the teachers and English is not learnt as it should be learnt by the students in the schools.

The standard of English is deteriorating fast. If we compare the graduates of today with the graduates of a few decades back, we can understand the marked difference between them. The graduates of a few decades back had better English knowledge, better application of skills and better skill in creative writing. But these days we don't see such standards or quality in our students. The conditions under which English is being taught in the schools these days are far from satisfactory. Teachers and students encounter various problems in teaching and learning of English. The worst sufferers in this regard are the low achievers, slow learners, the learning disabled etc.

However, the long period of exposure to English that our students have, enables them to have certain degree of familiarity with the sentence patterns. They have a limited stock of vocabulary also. With the words and the phrases that they know, the students have some limited ability to write in English, even though they are not able to speak in English. The conditions under which English is taught and learnt and the reasons for the poor performance of students in English are discussed below. The problems encountered in the teaching and learning of English can be enumerated as under:

1. Lack of clear-cut policy.
2. Little understanding of aims.
3. Lack of competent teachers
4. Faulty methods
5. Defective examination system
6. Crowded classes
7. Poor infrastructure
8. Lack of audio visual aids
9. Unsuitable textbooks
10. Variation in English syllabus
11. Improper correction work
12. Inadequate supervision
13. Reduction in the number of periods
14. Interference by parents
15. Interference of mother tongue
16. Lack of research

## LACK OF CLEAR-CUT POLICY

It is admitted by everyone that the standard of English has gone down in our schools and colleges. Lack of clear-cut policy is one of the reasons for the decline in the standard of English in schools and colleges. The Study Group on Teaching of English (1971) observes, "There have been frequent changes in government policy towards the teaching and learning of English in several states."

They further report that we have examples of more than one state where, only a few years ago, English was taught as a compulsory language and, however low the competence attained, pass marks had to be secured in the English paper in order to get through the High School examination. Today, largely because of the mounting concern caused by an alarmingly high percentage of failure in the subject at different end-of-the year and school leaving examinations, the governments have decreed that success in English should no longer be considered essential for admission to the under-graduate courses at the university.

Educationists, politicians and journalists express different views on the place and importance that English should be given in the school as well as college curriculum. Views expressed by these people outside the institutions do have their impact in the classroom teaching learning process. It is time that Government should lay down a clear-cut policy regarding the place and importance of English in school and college curriculum for an effective study of the English language. A national policy in this regard will mark a milestone in the effective teaching and learning of English in our country.

**Suggestions for Improvement**

National policy regarding the place of English in the school curriculum must be very clearly defined. It should not be vague. Similarly, the educational objectives of teaching English at the various stages of education must be clearly specified and the teachers should try to realise them. A clear-cut policy will help the educators to frame the syllabus and to enrich it accordingly with appropriate linguistic items to develop the skills of the students in listening, speaking, reading and writing.

## LITTLE UNDERSTANDING OF AIMS

Unfortunately, the average Indian teachers of English do not have any real understanding of the aims of teaching English in their day-to-day works. The teachers in the school teach English and the students learn English but none of them is fully clear about the real aim of teaching-learning English. The different items in the syllabus are covered in the class. The teachers and the taught consider English as a knowledge subject and not as a skill subject. The aim of the teacher is to enable his students to get through the examination. The teacher simply enables the students to master answers for some set questions important from the examination point of view.

In most of the schools, English is not taught as a skill subject as it ought to be taught but as a knowledge subject. As a result, the students are not able to acquire the expected proficiency in the linguistic skills that really matter. They are not able to express themselves in English. They develop no love for reading books in English. None of the four skills is adequately developed in students even at the end of the year. The teacher is like a sailor who does not know his destination and the students are like a rudderless ship drifting along anywhere ashore.

**Suggestions for Improvement**

Teachers should understand fully the different aims of teaching English. They should teach the language keeping the fundamental aims of teaching in view. All the aims i.e. listening, speaking reading and writing are equally important. Teachers should give due importance to each skill and teach the learners accordingly. Teachers should enable the learners to use the language in their day-to-day life situations.

## LACK OF COMPETENT TEACHERS

As is the teacher so are the students. Many teachers of English who are now teaching English subject are not competent. Only a few of them are really competent for teaching English subject. They are not able to pronounce the words properly with proper stress. They don't have the required command over English. Most of them are basically maths teacher or science teacher or social science teacher. In addition to their subject i.e. maths or science or social science they teach English subject also. These teachers are selected on the basis of their subjects studied upto BA., or B.Sc., level.

In this context, the English Review Committee appointed by U.G.C. in 1965 said, "There is a shortage of teachers. Those available have just passed the school final examination, having themselves studied English in a village school for 4 or 5 or 6 years. They have little idea of correct usage, and not at all of correct pronunciation. Their vocabulary is limited as is their reading."

Teachers of English are not fully equipped to discharge their duties in an effective manner. Some teachers are of the opinion that no specialised training is needed to teach English language. Teachers who did not study English methodology in the training college are entrusted with the task of teaching English. Such teachers cannot do full justice to their teaching. They cannot devise their instruction so as to reach out to all the learners. When the teachers are incompetent, the low achievers, the slow learners and the learning disabled in the class will suffer a lot. Teachers who studied English methodology in the training colleges also take to routine methods on their entry into the profession.

It is a fact that most of the teachers of English themselves are not aware of the latest techniques of teaching English. Their knowledge of the language is insufficient and their pronunciation is defective. As professor V.K. Gokak has pointed out: "The foundational years for the teaching of English in schools are in the hands of teachers who neither know enough English nor are familiar with the latest and far-reaching developments in the pedagogy of English". According to the Report of the Study Group (1971), there is a grave shortage of trained and fully qualified teachers of English at almost all stages of the educational system.

The teacher's skill and personality play a key role in creating conducive conditions for learning. He should be proficient in the language. His knowledge of English and his expertise in methods and techniques of teaching English should be of a reasonably high standard as Robert Lado says, "The language teacher must be educated, at least to the level of his peers. He must know the target language well enough to be imitated by his students". Wilkins is right when he observes, "It should be unrealistic to expect a teacher to set objectives which he himself is not capable of reaching. A teacher who himself has difficulty in speaking the language he teaches, is not going to succeed in giving his pupils a command of spoken English."

Now a beginning has been made by the Government of Tamil Nadu in this regard. They are appointing English teachers to teach English only at upper primary and secondary levels. It will not be long before we reap the fruit of this effort.

Since the teacher occupies a pivotal position in school education, we should have the right type of teacher to teach English. In addition to a rich background of English language and literature, he should be proficient in the latest techniques of teaching the language and should also have a knowledge of phonetics. The teachers of English should be given required training for improvement of their own English. Refresher courses should be organised for them whenever the syllabus is changed. It should be made compulsory for the teachers to attend such refresher courses. When there is new recruitment, only English teachers i.e. teachers with English as basic qualification should be recruited to teach English from Std vi onwards as it is now being done in the state of Tamil Nadu. Those who are good at English and have studied English methodology at B.Ed., level should be selected. The teachers who have additional qualifications acquired from RIE or CIEFL should be given preference in selection. These measures will certainly improve the situation.

## FAULTY METHODS

The translation method which is most wasteful is still followed in most of the schools in India. The new approaches i.e. structural and situational are not popular among our teachers. Though grammar and composition find a place in the English syllabus, most of the teachers don't know how to teach grammar and composition. Some teachers waste their time by giving undue importance to grammar. Undue emphasis on grammar does in no way, help in developing the four basic skills of the language learning. Composition is merely dictated by the teachers. They do not provide for creative writing. This type of teaching should be eschewed by the teachers and the teachers should strive hard to enable the students to speak, read and write English perfectly.

Translation method simply ignores all the aspects of learning a language. The teacher feels that he has completed a lesson once he finishes the translation of the lesson into the regional language. The teacher encourages the students for cramming the materials. In short, grammar is either neglected or over emphasised, the composition is dictated, the textbook is translated into mother tongue and the entire emphasis is on passing the examination through the magic wand of cramming. F.G. French permits the use of mother tongue in the classroom for explaining the meaning of the words but he insists that the teachers should go back into English as quickly as possible. But in our schools, this method is never followed.

Oral work which is the soul of any good method is neglected in our schools. The students do not get any opportunity to hear or speak the language. No oral practice is provided to the students in adequate manner. As a result, they cannot construct even a few sentences on their own. Nor can they speak a few sentences without mistakes in logical sequence. Even though there is provision for aural, oral and communicative practice in the English syllabus, the teachers just go about the job in a routine way or they ignore it altogether. They simply enable the students to cram answer to certain set questions and the students pass the examination by such cram work. Despite their pass in the exam with high score, the students miserably fail to acquire any linguistic skill.

The translation method which is time consuming and wasteful should be replaced by aural-oral approach. Sufficient oral work should be carried out in the classroom. The students should be provided with opportunities for expression. Most of the teachers in schools use this faulty method. Just to acquaint them with the latest techniques of teaching English orientation programmes can be organised. Inservice training programmes should also be arranged to enable the teachers to know the effectiveness of various methods in teaching English. Teachers who have done research in English education may be asked to provide orientation to the serving English teachers at Block or Taluk or district level. Moreover, teachers should be sent for special training courses in pronunciation.

## DEFECTIVE EXAMINATION SYSTEM

In any educational system, the type of examination influences the method of teaching to a considerable extent.

The existing examination system is to be blamed for some of the defects that have crept in. Teachers have tuned their teaching and the students have tuned their learning examination oriented. They do practise everything for the sake of examination. The paper setter sets the question paper which tests the crammed knowledge of the students. The test items in the question paper do not provide for measuring the basic skills acquired by the students in learning the language.

There is no examination to measure the skill of the students in spoken English. Though there is aural-oral test for the higher secondary students in the state of Tamil Nadu, the teachers and the students go about the aural-oral test in casual way. They do not give much importance to the test and the teachers do not take the required efforts to develop the aural oral skill in students. Thus the important aspect of learning the language is ignored. There is hardly any learning in the real sense of the word.

Under the present examination system, student can get through the examination with reasonably good marks if he cares to remember answer to certain stock questions. Some of the students are even unable to read the prescribed textbook. They simply learn by rote the essays and the questions and answers prepared by their teachers or found in their commercial guides and workbooks. The result is that though the students succeed in the examination, they do not have any practical command over the language. They can neither speak good English nor write correct English. The standard of spoken English in schools is deplorably poor and one of the reasons that can be ascribed for this state of affair is that there is no oral test.

The examination system in English should be oriented to teaching and not vice versa. The examination system should be revamped keeping in view the aims of teaching English in India. Examination should discourage cramming. There should be examinations to test the different skills of the students. Then there will be real teaching and learning of English. It is much encouraging to note that new style question papers have been introduced at the schools in most parts of the country thanks to the impact of evaluation units in the states and the institutes of English.

## CROWDED CLASSES

Owing to population explosion, classes have become overcrowded. There is no scope for individual attention. The number of students sitting in a class varies from sixty to eighty. In some aided schools, the number sometimes touches ninety. It is unreasonable to expect the teachers of such classes to pay individual attention to the students. As a result, the teachers are not able to do full justice to their duty and work. English is such a skill subject that it requires the teacher to pay individual attention to the students.

Even now there are students from illiterate families. Such students and other students like the low achievers, slow learners and the learning disabled require individual attention of the teachers for learning the language properly. Correct pronunciation, stress, intonation etc cannot be taught properly to the students in the overcrowded classes. The teacher cannot check whether the students have learnt these items correctly. The teacher cannot understand where the student is weak and he cannot take appropriate remedial measure to circumvent the weakness. Teachers cannot provide adequate drill and practice in large classes.

To overcome this problem the class strength should be limited to forty. The overcrowded classes should be bifurcated. When the classes are bifurcated, the question of appointing additional teacher arises. The Government doesn't sanction additional post. So most of the schools are not in favour of bifurcating the existing classes. English handling teachers are scared of valuing the papers. The English teachers of larger class have a tendency to shift to another school where there is poor strength. It is a common phenomenon found among the Government school teachers.

In a developing country like India we are constrained to accommodate more students in a single classroom. The teacher pupil ratio is also high. But efforts should be made to decrease the number of students. Where the strength is alarming, government should think of sanctioning additional posts. For grammar and composition work the teacher should form groups comprising lesser number of students. This will make the correction work easier and possible to the teacher. Further, the teacher should follow the techniques that have been verified to be effective for teaching larger classes, e.g. choral drills, group method.

## POOR INFRASTRUCTURE

Proper infrastructure is very essential for effective teaching and learning of English. The physical conditions under which English is being taught are unfavourable for optimum learning. There are schools with no good teaching arrangements. In the some schools, the classrooms are dark and not properly ventilated. In some cases, the rooms are separated by using bamboo screens. The noise from the neighbouring class disturbs the teacher and students. Neither the teacher not the students can concentrate properly with the blackboard that never allows the chalk to ride on it smoothly and with the chalk that breaks frequently it is a constant struggle for existence for the teachers in the poorly maintained schools. Fund is provided to Government schools under SSA scheme for improvement of infrastructures. But no such fund is provided to aided schools where 60% of the students are pursuing their study.

Infrastructure includes not only the well furnished classroom but also teaching materials such as chalk and blackboard, audio visual aids, library and language laboratory. Most of the schools do not have appropriate and adequate books for the use of the students. There are many books available in the open market which adorn the stacks in the library of matriculation schools. There are many books for reading practice, pronunciation practice and conversation practice. Such books do not find a place in the library of most of the schools. Even in such schools where the strength is less, the teachers are not able to provide above practice for want of adequate books for the use of the students. Unless the infrastructure is strengthened, it is not possible to ensure effective teaching learning of English.

The existing infrastructure should be strengthened. Proper and adequate buildings, adequate classrooms, classroom furniture, adequate black boards, a good library with books for learning English should be ensured. The school authorities should see to it and the inspecting officers i.e. AEO or DEO or CEO should check whether the school inspected has adequate infrastructure. If there is no adequate infrastructure they should make a mention of it in the inspection report. The provision of furniture grant, building, grant, science grant etc, may be extended to the aided schools also.

## LACK OF AUDIO-VISUAL AIDS

Most of the schools are not properly equipped with audio-visual aids such as flash cards, charts, pictures, models, filmstrips, gramophone records, tape recorders etc. which facilitate language learning. Flash cards, pictures and charts are very essential to provide drill and practice in oral reading and to build up basic vocabulary. Basic sentence patterns can be taught through charts. Substitution table charts can be used by the teachers to give drill practice in sentence patterns. What a visual presentation can do any amount of words cannot do. The visual effect will facilitate retention of the words and patterns in the memory of the students.

Film strips, linguaphone and tape recorders are necessary to provide speech practice to the students. Film strips are available in large number to teach English. They are very useful to teach pronunciation to students. There are film strips showing the tongue and lips position to pronounce vowels, diphthongs, consonants and certain words., By using the film strips the teacher can teach the students how to pronounce vowels, diphthongs, consonants and certain words. Tape recorder is an extremely useful aid to provide speech practice to students. A number of audio cassettes are commercially available to provide drill and practice in pronunciation, stress, intonation etc. Now a days we have VCD and DVD players

Realising the inadequacy of audio visual aids in schools, union government is now extending financial assistance to teachers under SSA scheme at the rate of Rs. 500/- per teacher every year for all the teachers handling classes upto std VIII to prepare or buy the required teaching aids to teach their subjects. This financial assistance is known as Teaching Learning Material (TLM) grant. Use of teaching aids provides for pleasant experience in the teaching learning process. They facilitate both instruction and retention. Use of audio visual aids is more required and more effective for low achievers and slow learners whose span of attention is short.

As for audio visual aids, the English teacher should make the best use of the blackboard by appropriate drawing and sketching on it. He should know how to prepare flash cards, charts etc. He should be always on the look out to collect relevant pictures which may help him in illustrating is lesson. Schools should be equipped with gramophone recorders, tape recorders and film projectors. English teachers should be given training to handle the different types of sophisticated aids. They should know how to use CD ROM and VCD to provide practice in pronunciation and conversation. They should also be acquainted with the libraries from where tape, CD Roms and VCD can be borrowed by the institution for teaching English.

## UNSUITABLE TEXTBOOKS

The prescribed English readers and the textbooks are sub-standard. No doubt these textbooks have been written by CIEFL and NCERT. The books have been adopted by the school boards of some states. In some states like Tamil Nadu they have their own Textbooks society. The English textbooks have many defects in them. They are unsuitable to the level of the students. A number of students find themselves in troubles while reading these books. A good English textbook will make the students read, not dread. The subject teachers also find many shortcomings in them. In the hands of average teachers these books miserably fail to deliver the goods.

The students are hardly attracted by the subject matter contained in the book. The subject matter is hardly related to the surrounding environment of the learners. The vocabulary and the structures also present difficulties to the learners. They are not in tune with the mental level of the learners. The subject matter is also beyond the experience level of the students. The difficulty of the language adds to the difficulty of the subject matter. Guy-Boas writes, "The only persons equipped to choose these books are school masters who really know the fodder suited to their flock."

Another shortcoming is that no attention has been paid to the selection and gradation of structures in writing the textbooks. Vocabulary has been graded from year to year but the authors of these books do not take pains to see that it is properly used in a manner to facilitate the grasp by the students. Some of the words which are sought to be taught appear only once in the text. They have laid more stress on the subject matter than on the teaching of the language. As a result, the teachers pay more attention to the subject matter rather than to the language. The illustrations in these books are few and leave much to be desired. There are no practice exercises to teach the language to the students. There are only testing exercises. But in the latest textbooks of English efforts have been made to provide for practice exercises. It is much encouraging to note that the latest textbooks published by the NCERT and CBSE have been prepared systematically and are free from the drawbacks pointed above.

The textbooks of English should be of very high standard. Highlighting this problem prof. V.K. Gokak says, "Either because of the distribution of patronage or because of fear of charges of favouritism, a Reader which is an organic part of one series is prescribed for a certain standard and it is followed by a Reader from another series. Books are prescribed which bear no relevance to the needs of pupils at that stage."

English textbooks need improvement in selection and gradation of vocabulary, good printing, genuine illustration, suitable subject matter, language and style, exercises and glossary relevance and abridgement of English stories to suit Indian conditions. Students workbooks, teacher's Handbook, supplementary Readers and necessary audio visual materials like charts, records and tapes should accompany the textbooks. These will go a long way in promoting effective teaching learning of English.

### Suggestion for Improvement

Textbooks written by CIEFL and NCERT experts can be used in schools throughout the country. Wherever the states have their own Textbook society, textbooks should be written in accordance with structural approach and should contain appropriate pictures and exercises. Graded linguistic materials should find a place in the textbooks. Efficient English teachers and research workers should be entrusted with the task of writing English textbooks. This will improve things further.

## VARIATIONS IN ENGLISH SYLLABUS

The prescribed syllabi for different classes are far from satisfactory. They are not related to the surrounding environment of the learner. Even after passing, the learners can hardly make use of anything learnt by them in their real life situations. In the schools, the students learn many essays, stories and letters but in real life situations, they are not able to write a simple application. Even if they attempt, it is full of mistakes which amuse others. In the latest English syllabus prescribed by the Government of Tamil Nadu, desirable attempts have been made to include life skills in English syllabus. Development of life skills should find a place in the English syllabus throughout the country.

There is no single syllabus for the whole country in India. Our educational system is not nationalised. It is in the concurrent list. All the central schools and the school in some of the states adopt the NCERT books. There are also states which have their own syllabus and textbooks. So there is a variation in the English syllabus in terms of skills coverage and development of language skills. At present there are three different stages at which the teaching of English is introduced. The variation in syllabus results in variation in achievement and in skill attainment. The right way to tackle this problem is to design the syllabus with clearly stated objectives right from the level at which English is introduced to the level at which English ceases to be a compulsory subject in curriculum.

If there is uniform syllabus throughout the country, it will certainly yield good result. Now the syllabi vary from state to state. It is important to ensure that there is a uniform syllabus in a particular state. A beginning has been made in this regard in the state of Tamil Nadu. Now the Government of Tamil Nadu has appointed textbook committees to frame uniform syllabus for each subject for all the types of schools in Tamil Nadu. Other states also may fall in line with Tamil Nadu to ensure uniform syllabus in their states.

## IMPROPER CORRECTION WORK

In the teaching of English language, correction work is of great importance. Correction work enables the teacher to understand how far his teaching has reached out to all learners, what are the areas where the students have not done well, what are the concepts yet to be clarified and strengthened and who are lagging behind in the learning. But in the schools we find that very little attention is paid to correction work. The school authorities don't bother about the correction work. They simply allot the same number of periods to English teachers as they do to other subject teachers. The workload on account of correction work is not taken into consideration. In their over busy schedule of work, the English teachers are not able to do full justice to their duty of correction.

The large strength in the classes is another reason for improper correction work. In some classes there are eighty to ninety students. In such classes, the teacher cannot carry out the correction work. Whenever the teacher provides the practice exercises, he is not able to correct or check the answers of the students. The alarming strength of the class makes it an impossible task. Even the whole period will not be sufficient to complete the correction work. As a result, the teachers resort to other means of correction which are highly improper. All this results in determination of standard. To overcome this problem all the exercises done by the students should be corrected properly and the mistakes committed by the students should be pointed out to them with proper corrections.

Correction work should be understood in its real perspectives by the school authorities. Number of periods should be allotted to English teacher taking into consideration the workload of correction. Teachers should pay more attention to correction works, point out the mistakes made by the students and provide the correct spellings or usages whatever the case may be. This will provide for reinforcement to the students. These measures will certainly improve the whole situation and help the teachers to teach English language in an effective way.

## INADEQUATE SUPERVISION

"The supervision of English teaching in schools has continued to be neglected, with hardly any trained specialist engaged in this task. The Head of the school normally supervises the work of the English teacher. Sometimes, the Head is conservative. He tries to poke his nose into the class affairs of the English teacher. Some Heads cherish the fault finding attitude without suggesting any solution for the problem. In most cases, the Head is not acquainted with the techniques of teaching English as he is from other discipline. His unnecessary interference and his unwanted criticism dishearten the teacher. The result is that the teachers receive no guidance in their teaching. They just carry on the work following the traditional method of teaching the language.

### Suggestions for Improvement

The Education Department should make provision for effective supervision of English teaching in schools. As and when they inspect the schools periodically, they can take language experts with them to supervise the teaching of English there. This will enable the experts to understand the strength and weakness of the teachers and to provide on-the-spot guidance to teachers for improving their teaching competence.

## REDUCTION IN THE NUMBER OF PERIODS

The number of periods allotted to the teaching of English has been drastically reduced to make room for the study of some other subjects that have been introduced at the school level. At high school level, seven periods per week have been allotted for English. At higher secondary level, seven periods per week have been allotted for each subject whereas for

English only four periods per week have been allotted. Within this limited periods, the teachers find it very difficult to cover the syllabus and to provide adequate drill and practice for development of linguistic skills in their students. They have to rush through to complete the syllabus and to make revisions.

**Suggestions for Improvement**

It is not possible to raise the number of periods allotted to the teaching of English, but the teachers can overcome this problem to some extent by reducing the use of mother tongue in the classroom so that students will get adequate practice in listening to English. To provide adequate drill and practice, the teacher can make use of additional instruction time. This will facilitate the learning of the low achievers, slow learners etc.

## INTERFERENCE BY PARENTS

Interference of the parents in the work of the teachers hinders the teaching learning process to a considerable extent. When the teachers make some effort to apply new and innovative techniques of teaching English, they have to face a set back in the form of interference of the parents whose children are studying there. Some parents are highly orthodox and conservative. There are parents who still attach undue importance to formal grammar as they were taught like that in their school days. They do not approve of the teaching of applied grammar, functional grammar and transformational generative grammar. If the teachers spend more time on oral drill and practice, the parents feel as if nothing had been taught. They judge the teachers' work on the basis of the written exercises only, corrected and valued. This undue interference of the parents hampers the teaching learning process.

**Suggestions for Improvement**

Teachers should try to provide aural-oral practice without any decline in the quantum of the written work. Teachers can make use of additional instructional time for this purpose. When there is PTA meeting, the teachers can apprise the parents of the new and innovative techniques that they are going to apply and the specific instructional objectives they are going to achiever. Once it is properly explained to them, the parents will certainly understand and they will extend their ostent approbation to the innovations of the teachers. Once they come to know the learning outcomes in course of time, they will definitely refrain from interference.

## INTERFERENCE OF MOTHER TONGUE

- No two languages are alike. It is rather difficult to find the exact equivalents of English language in Hindi or in any other regional language. There are 26 alphabets in English, 33 in Hindi, 35 in Punjabi and 30 in Tamil. These alphabets are used to produce all the sounds in the respective languages. It confuses the minds of the learners especially the low achievers and the slow learners.
- Hindi, Punjabi and Tamil are phonetic languages. Their spoken system and written system are the same. But English is not a phonetic language. So the learners of English, especially the slow learners and the learning disabled face a number of problems while reading or writing it. A few consonant sounds of English are not found in Hindi. e.g. the initial sound in the words 'thinks', 'then', the sound occurring in the middle of the words, measure, treasure. The sounds of this type pose problems for the learners who learn English in India.
- Stress, intonation and rhythm of English and the regional languages of India and Hindi differ widely. That also creates problems for the young learners of English in India. Also, the sentence patterns in English and our mother tongue are quite different. In Hindi and in Indian regional languages we use subject, object and verb pattern but in English it is subject + verb + object.
- Interrogative sentences in English and in Indian languages are different. In English, the interrogative sentences start with a question word, but in Indian languages the interrogative sentences start in a simply way. In Hindi an adjective undergoes a change according to the number or gender but in English it does not change. The verb changes according to the gender in Hindi but in English it does not.

- ❖ The structural words of English and Indian languages are not equivalents. The students' habit of producing sounds in mother tongue tells upon their English pronunciation. So we find striking variations in pronouncing English sounds from state to state. This hinders the effective learning of English.

**Suggestions for Improvement**

Teachers should make the students understand that no two languages are alike. The teacher should point out the dissimilarites found between English and Indian languages. Sound systems i.e. consonants and vowels pertinent to English only should be indicated to the students with adequate examples. To teach stress, intonation and rhythm the teacher should provide a good model. If he is not able to set himself as a good model, he should resort to the use of tape recorders. Then only students can be enabled to learn the correct stress, intonation etc. The difference between English and Indian languages in sentence formation and in the uses of adjective and verbs should be expounded to the students with examples from both the languages. These measures will minimise the negative effect of mother tongue on learning of English.

## LACK OF RESEARCH

Teaching learning process needs continuous overhauling. The drawbacks in the teaching learning process need immediate solutions to avert further deteriorations. Research is the means of arriving at scientific solutions. Teachers are the right people who can experiment with the students and come out with tangible solutions for the problems of the students. He who teaches the same thing in the same way year after year cannot be said to be a good teacher. A good teacher is one who is always on the look out for introducing innovative ways in his teaching. In this fast developing world, where knowledge explosion is taking place in every sphere, research on the part of the teachers is very essential. But the teachers of today are not able to carry on any research work. Many study hard to become teachers but once they become teachers they cease to study any more. Tagore says, "A lamp cannot burn another lamp unless it keeps burning". Without further study no teacher can plunge into any research work. Lack of research is one reason for continuance of the traditional method of teaching.

**Suggestions for Improvement**

As far as possible, teachers should be encouraged to carry on research works in their day to day working in the schools. They can undertake as many action researches as possible. When the research reports are published in the UGC or NCERT journals, the researchers should be adequately awarded. This will motivate the English teachers to make further probes into the teaching learning process. They can apply various types of educational and instructional technologies in the teaching learning process and their effectiveness on the achievement of the students can be assessed. They can attempt studies on the application and effectiveness of innovative instructional strategies. NCERT may provide fund for some projects. Research aptitude and attitude on the part of the teachers will certainly improve things.

## SUMMARY

The conditions under which English is taught in Indian schools differ from state to state and from one type of schools to another. English is taught under favourable conditions in public schools, Anglo. Indian schools and in some of the Matriculation schools whereas the conditions under which it is taught in most of the schools in any state for that matter are not favourable.

A glance at the present situation brings to light the sorry state affairs. Everybody is after the examination. A student doesn't bother about acquiring real knowledge of learning of the language. He makes all possible efforts to succeed in getting the diploma or the degree. What he wants most is score, not knowledge or skill.

The conditions under which English is being taught in the schools these days are far from satisfactory. Teachers and students encounter various problems in teaching and learning of English. The worst sufferers in this regard are the low achievers, slow learners, the learning disabled etc.

Mr. Ronald Mackin's paper on "The Teaching of English in Difficult Circumstances" is of special relevance to the teaching of English in India. He says, "The old-fashioned type of benches and desks which restrict movement; the bad light; the noise from neighbouring classes which may be separated from them by nothing more than a bamboo screen; insufficient provision for their subject in the time-table; lack of aids of all kinds; interference from parents or dominating conservative Headmaster; and finally, the requirements of an examination system which places a premium on the written language and consequently seems to favour the grammar-grinder of the old school."

# 3

# Principles of English Language Teaching

Teaching is not an easy task as it appears. A teacher has to keep in mind the aims and objectives of teaching the particular language, need and interest of his pupils, the environmental situation in which the teaching learning process takes place etc. Success of a teacher largely depends on good planning and mastery in the subject to be taught. Hence, to help the teacher accomplish this arduous task with a reasonable success, some principles have been designed on the basis teachers' experiences, traditions and research findings. These principles provide some guidelines to the teachers as to what methods should be adopted in the classroom to optimise the outcome of the teaching learning process.

A good teacher always wants to make his teaching as effective as possible. He wants his students to attend the class properly, listen to him keenly and try to grasp what he teaches in the class. The principles evolved by the educators enable the teacher to carry on his task of teaching efficiently by showing him the path to be followed and keeping him on the right track. They check him not only from going astray but also optimise the achievement of the teacher in the process of teaching.

## GENERAL PRINCIPLES OFTEACHING

There are a few principles of teaching which are of general nature. They are:

1. Principle of definite objectives

2. Principle of model presentation
3. Principle of selection of material
4. Principle of activity
5. Principle of correlation
6. Principle of child centredness
7. Principle of cooperation
8. Principle of planning
9. Principle of individual differences

**Principle of Definite Objectives**

While teaching any subject, the teacher should first of all fix up the general and the specific objectives of his teaching. Keeping this objectives in mind, the teacher should select the materials, employ the appropriate method and ensure the attainment of the objectives ultimately. Without definite objectives the activities of the teacher cannot be purposeful. The objectives constrain the students from deviating who may otherwise fail to achieve anything concrete.

The objectives of teaching may vary from subject to subject and from time to time. The objectives of teaching English are developing skills in listening, reading, speaking and writing. Earlier formal grammar was very emphasised. Nowadays functional or applied grammar is much emphasised. At present in India, much stress is laid on objectives of reading for comprehension and developing communicative competence. So in teaching English, the objective should be fixed first and then the teacher and the taught should make right effort for the attainment of the goals already fixed up. This will keep both the teacher and the students on the right track and enable them to work meaningfully.

**Principle of Model Presentation**

To make his teaching more effective the teacher should see that his presentation is really a model one in every way. The students look upon the teacher as a model. So the personality of the teacher, his behaviours, actions etc. should be a model one. The learners tend to imitate the teacher to a great extent. Whatever the teacher wants the learners to acquire, he should evince and follow in his life. Model presentation plays a key role in teaching English. His pronunciation, stress and intonation should be reasonably good. He should evince integrity, regularity, punctuality, truth, sincerity etc in his behaviour. These will enable his students to reach the goals of ideal life because the students look upon the teacher as a model for imitation and emulation. Further, these will make his teaching worthwhile and profit-yielding for humanity.

**Principle of Selection of Material**

The teacher should evince utmost care in selection of appropriate material in order to make his teaching reach out to all learners. Aims and objectives of teaching should be the governing criteria in selection of materials. The selected materials should be according to the liking of the learners and should be appropriate to the mental level of the learners. This will facilitate better acquisition and better information processing. As a result, the learning outcomes will be optimum. When the teacher uses appropriate materials in the teaching learning process, the slow learners will find the learning experience pleasant and this in turn, will account for better learning. A mere chalk and talk method cannot bring about desired results. Use of appropriate materials provides for linking the concept to be learnt with the existing knowledge or experience of the learners.

**Principle of Gradation**

Selection of appropriate materials, alone will not suffice. The selected materials should be graded properly. Gradation means logically deciding upon which item should come first, which item after that, which item to follow which item and which item at the end. In the gradation of materials easy and simple things should come first and difficult and complicated things should come afterwards. If there is no gradation of the teaching materials, it will cause frustration and ultimately disinterest in learning. It is more true so in case of the slow learners who get frustrated while learning complicated concepts. Gradation of materials provides the required rungs for the slow learners to make a steady progress without feeling any pinch. This presentation of materials in graded manner can make teaching learning process more effective.

**Principle of Activity**

There is no use in simply filling the minds of the learners with a lot of information. Mere passive listeners cannot become good students. Teaching-learning is a bipolar process which requires both the teacher and the taught to be active. Activity ensures involvement and doing on the part of the learners. The more the activity, the better is the teaching-learning process. Activity provides for retentivity. A concept learnt by doing tends to remain long in memory. As for the slow learners, the activity based teaching-learning is conducive for them. What the slow learners hear, they tend to forget; what they see, they tend to remember and what they do, they learn. An intelligent teacher ensures active participation of the students in the teaching-learning process. Active participation, in turn, drives away lethargy and boredom and promotes better learning. Above all, it creates interest in learning.

**Principle of Correlation**

Education prepares the children for future life. A good teacher correlates whatever he teaches with life. It makes the study more meaningful to the students. The students feel that they are being prepared for a better life. The teacher should correlate one subject with other subjects which the students are expected to learn. Correlation enables the students to understand the possible associations, existing similarities and dissimilarities and the far reaching implications. This kind of teaching is very useful for the slow learners. Tansley and Gulliford (1962) observe that the slow learners learn in a better way once they understand the possible association, existing similarities and dissimilarities.

According to John Dewey *"Education and life are two different names for the same phenomenon. Education which does not prepare the student for life is meaningless."* A teacher teaching arithmetic to the students should enable them to apply the knowledge of arithmetic acquired in school in their day to day life situations. A student applying his knowledge of mathematics in the market while purchasing feels happy and satisfied and he understands the use and value of the knowledge he possesses. This gives him a sense of pride and self-confidence. This sense of understanding of the value of the knowledge acquired provides required motivation to the students for further learning. Similarly, when a student uses English he learnt in the school in day to day life situations while conversing with his parents, relatives, friends or strangers, it gives him a lot of self confidence and a sense of pride. When the student feels that all the subjects he learns in the school prepare him for better life, it ensures better preparedness and active involvement on the part of the student for further learning.

**Principle Child Centredness**

Teaching should be child centred. It should not be allowed to remain teacher centred as it has been so far. Child centred teaching can reach out to the learners in a better way than teacher centred teaching. Child centred instruction is more conducive to the slow learners and their attentiveness increases when they are involved in child centred instruction. Child centred teaching means taking into consideration the liking and interest of the students in the teaching learning process. The interest will ensure active involvement of the learners in the teaching learning process. Then the learning becomes a pleasant activity. A concept in which the students have no interest should not be taught to them. A concept taught, where there is no learning readiness, will not reach out to the learners. The teacher should create interest in students by devising his instruction child centred and the interest created will ensure learning readiness and active involvement on the part of the students which are very essential for effective learning.

**Principle of Cooperation**

Teaching-learning is a cooperative venture which requires the involvement of all concerned for optimum attainment. For the teaching to be effective and successful, the teacher, the students, the Head of the institution, the parents and everyone else concerned should cooperate with one another. The coordinated effort of all concerned will facilitate a conducive atmosphere for a better teaching-learning process to take place in the classroom. The lack of cooperation of any one concerned will affect the teaching-learning process. In teaching the slow learners the principle of cooperation plays a vital role. It gives the slow learning students a sense of satisfaction that there are people who care for them. Cooperative teaching-learning gives them the feeling that they are no more the neglected ones. Further, it induces them to take initiative and effort to rise to the level of expectation.

**Principle of Planning**

The amount of care evinced in planning determines the degree of success in any venture. Proper planning ensures better and smoother process and better product. The principle of planning is the *sine* qua non of efficient teaching. A teacher should plan the entire teaching-learning activities before he enters the class. He should try to foresee the problems and he should think of appropriate solutions for the problems. A proper planning on the part of the teacher will ensure a performance par excellence. The teacher should plan properly and then he should work out his plan. Considerable flexibility should be maintained throughout the teaching learning process. He may mould things here and there to cater to the need and requirements of the learners in different situations.

**Principle of Individual Differences**

The problem that plagues every teacher in every subject at every grade level is how to teach a lesson to a class that contains students with different skills and learning rates. Accommodating instruction to student differences is one of the most fundamental problems of education and often leads to politically and emotionally charged policies.

The problem of accommodating student differences is so important that many educators have suggested that instruction be completely individualised so that students can work independently at their own rates. In the past twenty years, this point of view has led to the creation of individualised instructional programmes and computer assisted instruction. Simply speaking, individual difference refers to how the students differ from one another in a variety of ways, some important to instruction, some not.

Each of the many ways of accommodating student differences has its own benefits, but each introduces its own problems, which sometimes outweigh the benefits. Researches on various means of accommodating classroom instruction to student differences have been undertaken. However, before delving into the details, it will be apt on our part to consider what student differences are and which of them the teachers must take into account.

**Bases of Individual Differences**

From their first day in a school, students differ. They differ on several obvious dimensions that are of little importance to instruction, but they also differ in cognitive abilities and learning rates, which are of great concern to educators.

Many students enter L.K.G. or first standard knowing the alphabet and numbers upto ten, and some can already read a little. Others lack these skills. As time goes on, initial differences between students tend to increase, so that by High School or Higher Secondary School students may enter class with markedly different skills.

Differences in prior learning create the most serious problem in instruction (Tobias 1981, Corno and Snow 1986). For example, if a teacher presents a series of lessons on the discovery of America, it is of considerable importance to know how much students already know about the subject, how much they understand about the Renaissance in Europe, how well they can interpret maps and globes, and at the most basic level, how well they can read. If students are quite diverse in these skills, then the teacher must somehow take this diversity into account when presenting the lesson.

Another student difference, that teachers have to take into account is learning rate. Even if all the students begin class at same level, some are likely to learn more easily and rapidly than others. For example, a class learning a foreign language for the first time might begin with equal ignorance, but some students have an 'Ear' for foreign languages that others lack, and some have greater motivation to learn a foreign language than others. For these and other reasons, some students will learn more rapidly than their classmates.

A third difference that the teachers should be aware of is learning style (Dunn and Dunn 1978; Mossick 1984 and Carbo et.al., 1986). For example, some students learn best auditorily, some visually. Some work best alone, others with peers. Some need total silence to concentrate, others work well in a noisy room. Low achievement in academic performance may be due to the aforesaid factors. The instructor should, therefore, take care of such bases of differences and accordingly devise his instruction so as to cater to individual differences, especially to under achievers, low achievers etc.

## PSYCHOLOGICAL PRINCIPLES OFTEACHING

Psychological principles are those principles which are related to the psychology of the child. These principles are framed taking into consideration the interest, attitude aptitude and potentialities of the learners. They are formulated from the learners' point of view only. Application of psychological principles creates interest in students for learning. Where there is desire to learn, the learning becomes more effective and easier besides facilitating better information processing, longer memory storage and smoother recall.

### Difference Between General Principles and Psychological Principles

General principles enable the teachers to make the teaching-learning process more effective whereas the psychological principles make use of motivational techniques to gear up learning and to enhance achievement. General principles exercise influence on a wide range whereas the psychological principles work within limited range. General principles provide mere guidelines as to what to do and how to do but the psychological principles suggest suitable strategies or solutions for the problems.

### Important Psychological Principles

Some psychological principles deserve detailed explanation. Such important psychological principles are:

1. Principle of motivation
2. Principle of repetition and exercise

3. Principles of feedback and reinforcement
4. Principle of variety
5. Principle of rest and recreation
6. Principle of readiness
7. Principle of fostering creativity
8. Principle of sympathy and cooperation
9. Principle of self-learning
10. Principle of group dynamics.

**Principle of Motivation**

Teaching is a tripolar process which involves the interaction of the teacher, the students and the subject matter. Cooperation and proper rapport between the teacher and the students can facilitate better teaching-learning process. Now the concept of teaching has changed. The emphasis has been shifted from the teacher to the taught. So ensuring the cooperation and learning readiness of the learners is of primary importance to the teacher. He should ignite the spark of interest in students for the subject he is going to teach. To create interest the teacher can make use of various motivational techniques. A teacher's success in teaching is largely determined by how efficiently he makes use of motivational techniques. The children evince interest in their surroundings. So the teacher should provide the students with such learning materials that have relevance to classroom situation and life situation. The examples provided should bear relevance to life situations. This will make the learners become interested in learning the concept.

Before introducing the topic, the students should adequately be motivated towards the topic. This will ensure the required learning readiness on the part of the learners. This is especially very useful for the slow learners who are slow to catch on whatever is taught to them. Once they are motivated towards the topic, they will become interested in the topic and they will actively participate in the teaching-learning process. Active participation will, in turn, account for better acquisition. A change in the environment of the class will help to break the monotony. Adequate use of appropriate aids will add to the interest of the students. The teacher should apprise the students of the utilitarian value of English grammar, pronunciation etc. He can explain to the students how English can help them to choose a better career and how it can be helpful for securing a good job. These techniques will provide the require motivation to the students to learn English properly.

**Principle of Repetition and Exercise**

Repetition is very essential to drive home the main points. The teacher should repeat the main points so that the teachers will be able to grasp the concept in a better way. Repetition ensures not only assimilation but also retention. Exercises provide for the required drill and practice. Thorndike has verified the effectiveness of repetition and exercises in the learning process. Practice makes a man perfect. The students will learn best when they do or practise. Exercises provide for drill and practice and they pave the way for learning by doing. Tansley and Gulliford (1982), Ramar (1997) observe that repetition, review, drill and practice are very essential to accentuate the learning of the slow learners. For proper learning of the concepts taught, the slow learners need adequate repetition, review, drill and practice in the teaching-learning process.

For instance, while teaching Geometry, merely teaching that the sum of all the three angles of a triangle is equal to 180° is not sufficient. The slow learners will not be able to understand the concept. On the other hand, besides stressing the main point the teacher may ask the students to draw various triangles such as isosecles, equilateral and right angled triangle and ask the students to measure the angles of those triangles and find out the sum of all the three angles of a triangle. When they actually do the drawing and measuring, they will certainly understand that the sum of all the three angles of a triangle is equal to 180° in all three cases. The teacher may repeat again by giving some more examples of other triangles with different angles. This will ensure better acquisition of knowledge and longer retention.

**Principles of Feedback and Reinforcement**

In his instructional process a teacher should provide positive reinforcement to the learners. Positive reinforcement promotes learning. He should provide adequate feedback which is essential for better learning. The teacher should provide the knowledge of results side by side and as quickly as possible. This enables the slow learners to understand their weakness and strength. They can understand where they went wrong and they can relearn the concept and prepare themselves for further learning. Providing immediate feedback to the students enable the teachers to adjudge his own teaching. He can judge whether his instruction has reached out to all the learners and how far he has been successful in imparting instruction and then depending on the level of effectiveness of his teaching, he can modify or devise his instructional strategy accordingly. Further, constant encouragement also should be provided to the students as far as possible as it helps in developing a congenial atmosphere.

When the teacher puts a question to the whole class, he should encourage the students to come forward or to try to give the required response. When the students find it very difficult to give the required response, the teacher should refrain from adversely criticising the students branding them dull or hopeless. On the other hand, he should make them think critically by providing clues and examples. As they try and give the response, the teacher should provide positive reinforcement which will facilitate further learning. Positive reinforcement strengthens learning and facilitates further learning. Negative reinforcement hinders learning. Feedback provided at the right moment fosters self-confidence and creates interest in learning.

**Principle of Variety**

Variety is the spice of teaching-learning process. The teacher should make use of variety of ways in his classroom teaching. Using same method of teaching always should be avoided. The teacher should make use of variety in his instructional presentation as well as elucidation, depending on the concept taught, mood of the learners and the hour of teaching. Without variety teaching will be no better than a spiceless dish. Different methods at different times should be used for effective teaching-learning. Variety draws the attention of the students and creates interest in learning. Once the students become attentive and interested, their learning is better.

**Principle of Rest and Recreation**

The long hours of work and the complexity of the concept cause fatigue. Fatigue hinders learning. When the students are fatigue, no worthwhile information processing can take place. Hence, the learners must be provided with adequate rest and recreation during the schools hours. This not only refreshes their mind but also ensures better preparedness for further learning. Research works of Curtis, K. and Shaver J.P (1980) reveal that the attention span of the slow learners is relatively short. They lack concentration also. They cannot concentrate on the instruction of the teacher which is mostly verbal exposition for more than thirty minutes at a stretch. To provide rest and recreation the teacher can make use of digression technique by citing episodes from life situations related to the concept being taught. This will not only provide the learners with rest and recreation but also the examples cited will enable the learners to understand the concept in a better way.

**Principle of Readiness**

Learners must be ready to learn the concept to be taught. If the learners are not ready to learn the concept, the teaching however effective it may be, cannot yield fruits. Research into readiness for learning has shown that children's success in learning is often delayed by introducing them to instruction before they are able to benefit from it. Even now some of the teachers make their instructional presentation before the learners become ready. As a result, they become frustrated, bored, puzzled and lack confidence. Then it becomes all the more difficult to teach them when they do become ready to learn. It is therefore essential that teachers of young children and of slow learners should be aware of what readiness for learning entails and how readiness can be promoted. The teachers should assess certain vital factors which influence learning readiness before they decide upon any relevant strategy to teach the slow learners. The main factors which should be assessed are the learners' mental maturity, background of experience, special abilities and personal characteristics. The teachers should know that the intellectual development of children cannot be thought of as isolated from such things as memory, attention, concentration, emotional development and social background and experience.

**Principle of Fostering Creativity**

Fostering creativity is an essential requirement for effective learning. The teacher should foster creativity among the students. He should not encourage cramming or rote memory. When a student makes an innovative response, it should not be criticised. On the other hand, it should be appreciated and the teacher should point out to the whole class how creative the student or the response has been. This will induce other students also to think creatively. In composition exercises there is adequate scope for the students to express their creativity. Where there is such creative performance, the teacher should take notice of it and he should award marks liberally. Such creative performance can be read out to the whole class so as to inspire the other students to make adequate endeavour to embark on such venture.

**Principle of Sympathy and Cooperation**

The teacher should evince a sympathetic attitude towards students and a cooperative bent of mind in the school environment in general and in the classroom in particular. Inhibition and fear of authority hinder learning. Hence, it is the primary duty of the teacher to see that the students are neither inhibited nor afraid of him unnecessarily. An affectionate approach of the teacher can at times be more effective than his well planned instruction. The teacher should have adequate knowedge about the students, his abilities or disabilities, his home background and the circumstances under which he is pursuing his study. Keeping all these in mind, the teacher should be sympathetic and cooperative in dealing with the students. Teachers should act like parents away from home.

**Principle of Self-learning**

A good teacher should be appreciative of the initiative made by the student for learning anything. He should encourage the self efforts of the students. Self efforts made by the students will result in optimum learning. The teacher should teach in such a way that the students should develop the habit of self learning. Teachers should refrain from spoon feeding while teaching. The teacher may start with lecture method but he should slowly prepare the students for self-learning techniques. The teacher should remain in the background helping and guiding the students whenever and wherever they need some help or guidance. This principle induces the learners, especially the slow learners to set a goal for themselves and to strive hard to achieve that goal.

**Principle of Group Dynamics**

Children learn better in a group. They are able to develop such desirable qualities as tolerance, cooperation, sacrifice etc. The group exposure and interactions among the peers do have their own cumulative effect. The teacher should have a knowledge of group dynamics. He should try to cultivate among the learners a suitable type of group behaviour. For this purpose the teacher should do his job of teaching in such a way as to make his students well behaved in every type of situation both as an individual and as a group member. This will go a long way in cultivating right type of group behaviour in students.

Principles of teaching are, undoubtedly effective tools in the hands of efficient teachers. Competent teachers are able to put these principles into right use. The saying that *a bad workman quarrels with his tools* is true in case of incompetent teachers. The different principles of teaching can work wonders in the hands efficient teachers. The teacher trainees should develop a right insight into these principles and try to put them into use during their teaching practice. The application of these principles will make them better teachers in due course of time.

## THE MAXIMS OFTEACHING

Maxim is a general truth drawn from science or experience. Over the years various educationists have given numerous rules of conduct for teaching which may be called maxims. These maxims are true facts verified by the teachers on the basis of experience. These maxims are of universal significance and serve as useful guidelines to the teachers. Every teacher should have a thorough knowledge about these maxims and follow them in his instructional practice. This will enable the teachers to embark on his teaching venture with required self-confidence and accomplish the task with a considerable degree of success. The maxims that are of great importance are:

1. Known to unknown
2. Simple to complex
3. Concrete to abstract
4. Analysis to synthesis
5. Particular to general
6. Empirical to rational
7. Induction to deduction
8. Psychological to logical
9. Actual to representative
10. Near to far
11. Whole to part
12. Definite to indefinite

**Known to Unknown**

This maxim is based on the assumption that the students possess some existing knowledge. Teachers are to increase or develop this knowledge further. The teachers have to interpret the new knowledge in the light of the existing knowledge. This enables the learners to understand the link and the association between the existing knowledge, information in his mind and the new one being taught. The existing knowledge serves as a hook on which the new knowledge can be hung. Known is trustworthy and the unknown cannot be counted. So in his instructional practice, a teacher should proceed from known to unknown. This will enable the slow learners to relate the new concept being taught with the existing one in his mind. Otherwise he will be perplexed. Once the slow learners are enabled to understand the link between the new information and their existing knowledge, they will find the learning possible and fruitful. Suppose the teacher is teaching English grammar. While teaching sentence pattern, the teacher should link it with the parts of speech taught earlier. Similarly, while teaching word order, he should link it with the parts of speech and sentence pattern.

**Simple to Complex**

Classroom interaction is a formal teaching learning process where the teacher tries to teach and the students try to learn things. In this process of teaching, learning, the teacher should see that simple things are presented first to the students. Starting with simple things creates interest in learning. Once they become interested in learning, the students are bound to evince better attentiveness and readiness for learning. Then the complex concept can be introduced gradually in a graded manner. The encouragement provided and the confidence gained while learning simple things will sustain their interest for further learning. This will make them more receptive to the complex matter. On the other hand, if this maxim is discarded and the complex concept is introduced first, the students will become frustrated which will retard learning.

Simplicity or complexity of the subject matter should be determined on the basis of the learners' view point, not on the basis of teacher's opinion. For example, while teaching types of sentences, simple sentences should be taught first and then compound and complex sentences should be introduced.

**Concrete to Abstract**

Concrete things provides for visualisations whereas abstract things provide for speculations and imaginations. The slow learners find it very difficult to conceptualise abstract things. So concrete things should be taught first which can be understood by the students with ease. This initial understanding of concrete things will give the required learning readiness for learning the ensuing abstract things. Froebel said, *"Our lesson ought to start in the concrete and end in the abstract"*. For example, in teaching counting to the students, the teachers should first make use of concrete objects such as beads, stone etc, and then proceed to digits and numbers.

### Analysis to Synthesis

Analysis means breaking into convenient parts and synthesis means grouping the parts into a complete whole. A complex lesson can be made simple and easy for the slow learners by dividing them into many conceptual subunits. Once the students understand the conceptual subunits, they can understand the complex lesson in a better way. Analysis is essential for understanding and synthesis is a must for fixation. In teaching English, analysis of sentences should be taught first. This will enable the students to understand the different parts of a sentence. Once the learners have a reasonable knowledge about the constituent parts of a sentence, synthesis of sentences can be introduced. This will make the learning task easier for the students. Analysis provides the required foundation blocks for further learning.

### Particular to General

In teaching any subject, the teacher should first of all deal with particular things. The students should be enabled to understand the particular things first. Then on the basis of those particular cases, generalisations must be made. Suppose the teacher is teaching present continuous tense, he should first of all give a few sentences and make an explanation of them. Then on the basis of the sentences provided to the students the teacher should generalise that present continuous tense is used to denote an action that is taking place at the time of speaking. When such generalisations are made on the basis of particular cases, the students can understand the concept in a better way and they will learn to generalise things on their own in due course.

### Empirical to Rational

Empirical knowledge is based on observation and first hand experience whereas rational is based on arguments and explanations. Empirical is particular, concrete and simple. We can see, feel and experience it. Seeing things or feeling them is the first stage. It is followed by the stage of argumentation. Empirical refers to particular or specific statements whereas rational refers to more general statements. So the teachers should always proceed from empirical to rational. Rational needs more mental maturity than empirical. This maxim banks upon the previous knowledge of the students. What is within the purview of their experience is introduced first and then they are gradually led for making rationalities in generalisations.

**Induction to Deduction**

Induction means arriving at or drawing a conclusion from a set of examples. In induction, we study the examples first and then draw the governing rule from the examples. On the other hand, in deduction, the teacher gives the governing rule first and then he furnishes illustrative examples to drive home the governing rule. The latter requires more competence on the part of the students. The teacher should proceed from induction to deduction while teaching any subject. The slow learners find it easier to draw the rule from the examples than to learn the rule first. Suppose the teacher is teaching *Reported Speech* in English grammar, he should not go on explaining the governing rules or the procedures in the transformation. These abstract concepts will puzzle the slow learners. On the other hand, the teacher should provide concrete examples first. Then he should point out the parts that undergo changes and explain how they change. For each type the teacher should give a few examples and explain the transformation step by step. After explaining all the steps or the procedures in the transformation, the teacher should explain the governing grammatical rules and point out how they have been applied in the worked out examples. This will enable the students to understand in a better way.

**Psychological to Logical**

While teaching any subject, the teacher should first take into consideration the interest, aptitudes, capacities, level of intellectual development etc of the students. These should form the basis for selection of the subject matter. Then only the teacher should go on to logical arrangement. Without any psychological consideration, logical presentation or arrangement will be of no use. The psychological considerations are of more importance at early stages especially in case of the slow learners. Interest, aptitude and level of intellectual development play a key role in the learning of the students. Hence, the teachers should keep in mind the psychological factors before proceeding to the logical factors.

**Actual to Representative**

To effectuate better learning actual things or objects should be shown to the students as far as possible. Use of actual objects in the teaching learning process facilitates better learning. It provides for better understanding and clear conceptualisation. As a result of this concrete learning, the slow learners will be able retain the newly learnt information in their minds for a long time. Specially in the lower classes first hand information to the slow learners impresses them to a considerable extent. As they advance in learning, representative things in the form of pictures, models etc should be used. This will enable the students to visualise the actual object or process. That is why study tour is considered more important for the students. In the study tour, they see the actual things or processes and understand in a better way. At a safer stage when they see the representative of these things or processes, they will be able to visualise and conceptualise.

**Near to Far**

Normally students are able to learn well what is in the surroundings to which they belong. This warrants that the students should be taught about the things in their immediate environment. It will lay the foundation for further learning. Gradually they should be taught about those things which are far from his immediate environment. This will smoothen the teaching-learning process considerably. The children should be taught about home first before proceeding to the concept of street, bazaar, school and the city they belong to which is a distant environment for them at early stage. As far as the students are concerned, they are able to understand the things in their surroundings without much difficulties. The conceptual clarity provided by this learning facilitates their understanding of things in the far off environment. This maxim facilitates transfer and application of knowledge in students.

**Whole to Part**

In teaching, the teacher should try to acquaint the children with the whole lesson first and then the component portions of it may be dealt with thoroughly. The whole is more then the sum of the parts. This facilitates better understanding. Otherwise the children, especially the slow learning ones, will find it very difficult to understand the underlying sequence, coherence, and development of thoughts or concepts. This maxim holds good while teaching English to slow learners. At the early stages, children love to speak full sentences as they are exposed to full sentences in real life situation. So the children should be given full sentences first. From the sentence they will understand the constituent parts. In teaching a poem, the students should be acquainted with the whole poem first. Then they may be asked to grasp the poem stanza by stanza. This maxim holds good for the slow learners. This helps the teachers to teach better and the slow learners to learn better. They will understand the sequence, coherence and the development of the theme in a better way.

**Definite to Indefinite**

In teaching any subject, definite things provide for conceptual clarity and it gives the required confidence to learn the given concept. The slow learners' limited cognitive capacity also requires the definite things to be introduced first. So the definite things should be taught first and then the teacher should gradually proceed to indefinite things. Definite things and definite rules of grammar enable the slow learners to make a reasonable mastery of the subject. Learning of definite things paves the way for and facilitates the learning of indefinite things.

The maxims explained hitherto are only hints and guidelines for the teachers especially the ones dealing with children at early stage. These are most useful for the teachers teaching the slow learning children who constitute a sizeable portion of students population. The teachers should make use of these maxims in their teaching situations. If these maxims are applied in the instructional presentation, they will remain effective tools and yield better results.

## PRINCIPLES OF ENGLISH LANGUAGE TEACHING

English is taught both as a foreign language and as a second language in India. It is still a matter of controversy whether the learning of a second language is similar to the learning of the first language. There are some linguists who argue that the principles of first language teaching apply to the second language also. Robert Lado defines second language acquisition as *"acquiring ability to use its structure within general vocabulary under essentially the conditions of normal communication among native speakers at conversational speed"*. To put it more specifically, it refers to the acquisition of language skills to use the structure and content of the language as native speakers do.

There are certain basic principles which are essential for good language teaching. A foreign language teacher must always keep in his mind the basic principles of language teaching to make his teaching more effective. Application of these principles in the instructional process will make the instruction reach out to all the learners. Any language teaching not based on these principles cannot reach out to backward students like slow learners, the learning disabled etc. who are slow to "catch on" whatever is taught. Adequate knowledge and application of certain principles in the instructional process helps the teacher to teach the same language more effectively. The basic principles of teaching a second language are as follows:

1. Principle of naturalness
2. Principle of exposure
3. Principle of imitation
4. Principle of drill and practice
5. Principle of habit formation
6. Principle of oral approach
7. Principle of proper order and proportion
8. Principle of motivation and interest
9. Principle of selection
10. Principle of gradation
11. Principle of multiple line of approach

12. Principle of context and situation
13. Principle of accuracy and correctness
14. Principle of correlation with life
15. Principle of balanced approach

**Principle of Naturalness**

A child learns the mother tongue more easily because it is learnt in a natural environment. It is spoken in the family and the living environment of the child. But this is not the case with a foreign language. The child listens to the foreign language only in school. So he experiences considerable difficulty in learning the foreign language. To overcome this problem, the teacher should take effort to provide a natural environment for the child to learn the foreign language. Such natural environment provided to the children will tell upon their language acquisition. The teacher can provide natural environment as explained below:

(a) The teacher must talk to the students in the foreign language in the classroom, playground etc. The more the teacher uses the language, the easier the students will learn.
(b) He should encourage the students to converse with one another only in English without inhibition.
(c) He can arrange for group discussion, role play, elocution, simple play etc. These activities will provide for opportunities to use the language.

**Principle of Exposure**

The child learns the mother tongue more quickly because he has constant exposure to it. The people around the child speaks in mother tongue. The child listens to such speech and conversation and tries to use it to express its need and wish. So the teacher should provide ample opportunities to the students by using the English language more and properly in the classroom. This will give the students a better exposure to the language. The more they are exposed, the quicker they will learn. To provide better exposure to the students the teacher can take up the following measure.

(a) He should distribute pamphlets in English among the students and he can ask the students to go through them.

(b) The teacher can start English language club in the school and arrange for periodical programmes in which students should be trained to participate.

(c) Charts with slogans written in English can be displayed on walls and in the classrooms. This will enable the students to understand the slogan and the structural pattern.

(d) Slides in English can be shown to the students. This will facilitate reading and comprehension of the students.

(e) Now-a-days all the schools have TV and DVD player. So English movies can be played to the students. This will enable the students to learn correct pronunciation and intonation.

(f) The teacher should refrain from using mother tongue in the English class. Mother tongue should be used only when there is need and for instructional presentation and progressive explanation English alone should be used.

**Principle of Imitation**

Imitation plays a key role in learning any language. In fact, imitation is natural to man. In early childhood, the child learns the language through imitation. Whatever they see and whatever they hear, the small children tend to imitate. Sometimes the wrong habits of the parents and the wrong pronunciations of the teacher are also acquired by the children in this way. If a teacher's pronunciation is bad, his students at early stages of learning will pick up the same wrong pronunciation from him. Similarly, the bad handwriting of the teachers may also have adverse effect on his students.

So the teachers in charge of teaching small children should set themselves as good models. His pronunciation and his handwriting should be a model for the students for emulation by them. The teachers should possess exemplary classroom behaviour as well as social behaviours as the students look on him as their model. All these will have a lasting impact on the personality development of the children. It is therefore, very essential that really competent teachers should alone be recruited for teaching small children in schools.

**Principle of Drill and Practice**

Language learning is a habit forming process. Habits are formed through repetition. Repetition requires continuous drill and practice. Drill and practice plays a key role in acquisition of the basic skills of any language i.e. listening, speaking, reading and writing. The students should be able to use the language correctly though they may not know the rules of grammar. Robert Lado says, "*To know the language is to use its patterns of construction with appropriate vocabulary at normal speed for communication*".

Practice makes a man perfect. Practice ensures speed and accuracy. Language is rather a skill subject than a knowledge subject. Robert Lado rightly points out, "*The student must be engaged in practice most of the learning time. This principle has a psychological justification since other things being equal the quantity and permanence of learning are in direct proportion to the amount of practice*". In this regard, Fries recommends that eighty five percent of the allotted time should be devoted to practice and fifteen percent time should be utilised for explanation and comments.

Thompson and Wyatt write in their book 'The Teaching of English in India', "*The power of expression in a language is a matter of skill rather than of merely meanings or rules.*" In the learning of a language the students require a lot of practice and drill work. Only then they will be able to learn it properly. Language learning or teaching is not a knowledge subject, it is rather a skill subject like swimming, dancing, painting etc. So the learner will have to repeat and revise things in order to have mastery over the language. The various skills of language learning i.e. listening, speaking, reading and writing will be properly-learnt through practice and drill work. Otto Jesperson says, "*He who gets the tip of his finger dipped in the water three times in twenty weeks will never lean, how to swim.*" This indicates how far continuous practice is required for acquisition of language skills.

**Principle of Habit Formation**

According to Palmer, *"language learning is essentially a habit forming process, a process during which we acquire new habits"*. In language learning the following habits must be developed among the students:

(a) Habit of listening to sounds and distinguishing between sounds
(b) Habit of speaking with proper pronunciations, intonation and accent.
(c) Habit of imitating
(d) Habit or repeating
(e) Habit of learning correct spelling
(f) Habit of reading with articulation
(g) Habit of silent reading
(h) Habit of using grammar correctly
(i) Habit of using words in their proper content and in proper order.
(j) Habit of consulting a dictionary
(k) Habit of reading newspapers, journals, magazines, story books and so on.

**Principle of Oral Approach**

Oral work is of primary importance in teaching and learning a language. Language is more connected with ears and tongues than with eyes. If a student is proficient in speaking the language, he will automatically acquire the required skills in reading and writing because speaking leads to reading and writing. Moreover, whatever is learnt orally is remembered better and longer. So the teachers should make use of oral approach to an optimum level in English classes.

**Principle of Proper Order and Proportion**

A teacher should follow the proper order in teaching the four basic skills namely listening, speaking, reading and writing. Besides following the principle of proper order, teachers should follow the principle of proportion also. While teaching English language due importance should be given to each aspect or language skill. Palmer points out, *"All items in the whole range of the subject and aspects must receive an appropriate degree of attention so that the students knowledge of them may ultimately form a harmonious whole."*

**Principle of Motivation and Interest**

Teachers should not underestimate the impact of motivation and interest on teaching-learning process. Motivation plays an important role in learning a language. Motivation is the core of the language but motivation is not an easy task, when there is no internal drive for learning the language. Therefore, some special motivational techniques such as the following should be made use of by the teachers.

**(a) Arousing Techniques**

This category includes those techniques that arouse the students from a state of lethargy and sleepiness, inducing interest and curiosity. This activates the students to surge forward.

**(b) Expectancy Techniques**

To motivate a student there must be a predetermined goal to achieve and an expectancy to achieve that goal. The teacher should, therefore, place well defined goals before the students. This will motivate the students to strive hard to achieve that goal.

**(c) Incentive Technique**

This category includes techniques such as prize, praise, compliment, punishment etc. An encouraging word or an appreciative word from the teacher will motivate the students to learn with renewed verve and vigour.

Interest is of great importance in teaching-learning process. Language is learnt quickly when interest is in it. To create interest in students for language learning the teacher can make use of interesting methods like activity method and playway method in addition to a variety of teaching aids. These will not only create interest but also sustain interest in students for language learning.

**Principle of Selection**

In language teaching selection of language items is very important. Selection must be done by the teacher in respect of grammatical items, vocabulary and structures. While selecting the language items, the following points must be kept in mind.

(a) *Frequency*: Such words or sentences which have a high frequency of occurrence should be used.

(b) *Range of Applicability*: Every word has its range. Range shows the number of situations in which a word can be used. For example, *present* can be used in many situations.

He was present

They gave me a present

He presented me a book

He presented the paper well.

(c) *Language*: Words having more covering capacity should be selected. For example, the word cereal has a good covering capacity as it refers to wheat, rice, pulse etc.

(d) *Availability*: The teacher should use such words which refer to the objects or actions available or prevalent in the classroom environment or school environment or social environment. This will enable the students to pick up the words quickly.

(e) *Teachability:* The teacher should use such words which are easy from teaching point of view. Words differ in teachability. The word *flower* or *fruit* can be taught easily be showing a real one or by showing a picture of it or by drawing it on the blackboard. But it is difficult to teach abstract words such as *affection or tolerance.* While selecting words for teaching, the teacher should select such words which can be taught easily by making use of various devices.

(f) *Learnability*: Learnability refers to the ability of the students to learn the given language item. The teacher should select those items which are easy for the students to learn. The students will find the language items learnable if the selected language items are in accordance with his age and experience level. The teacher should bear in mind the above principles of selection while selecting language items to be taught to children.

### Principle of Gradation

Gradation means arranging the language items in order of presentation. Gradation involves grouping and sequence. The selected language items must be graded keeping in mind the level of difficulty and utility. In this context W.R. Lee observes, "*Teach first those sentences/structures the use of which can be made clear by means of visible actions in the classroom*". The basic principles of grading are as follows:

**(a) Principle of grouping**

According to the principle of grouping the items selected should be grouped on the basis of sound, situation, structure, sentence and meaning. This makes the process of learning easier. If the items are grouped on the basis of sound, it is called "*phonetic grouping*".

e.g. pay, bat, say sat etc.

When the grouping in done on the basic of situation, it is called "*lexical grouping*"

e.g. words connected with post-office post master, dak, letter etc.

If the basis of grouping is patterns of sentences, it is called "*grammatical grouping*".

e.g. This is my book That is your book etc.

When the selected items are grouped on the basis of meaning, it is called "*semantic grouping*".

e.g. shelter, hut, house, tent etc.

**(b) Principle of Sequencing**

Sequencing refers to what must come after what. Sequencing helps the teacher to decide which item should follow which items. There are three types of sequencing. They are as follows.

*Grammatical sequence* refers to which pattern or structure should follow which.

e.g. His is playing He is playing in the ground. ® He is playing in the ground now. ® He is playing football.® etc.

*Lexical sequence:* refers to which word should follow which.

e.g. sit, stand, come, go

or follows either, nor follows neither etc.

*Sematic sequence* refers to teaching the words of same meaning one by one in proper order.

e.g. We take *meals*. We take *breakfast*. We take *lunch*. We take *dinner*.

**Principle of Multiple Line of Approach**

While teaching a foreign language a teacher should adopt multiple line of approach which refers to judicious and rational selection of various approaches to teach a concept. It helps the learners and the teacher in many ways. Suppose the learners are to be prepared to write an essay on 'A Place of Historical Importance." First of all there should be a oral work and then the students may be asked to write a few sentences on that topic. Spelling practice related to the topic (required verbs, adjective etc.) should be given. While doing translation, sentences on the selected topic or a passage about the selected topic i.e. A Place of Historical Importance may be given. Thus our approach should be many sided in teaching a foreign language. Various approaches that may be used are social, functional, cultural, behavioural, phonetic, situational and structural. Multiple approaches facilitate the learning of slow learners.

**Principle of Context and Situation**

Language should be taught and learnt in appropriate context and situation. When it is done so, the students will be able to make use of it in their day-to-day life situations. Different language items such as vocabulary, structure etc. should be taught in the context of appropriate situations so that the students will find them very near to life. Eugene A. Nida observes, *"Language learning means plunging headlong into a series of completely different experiences. It means exposing oneself to situations where the use of language is required"*. It is therefore very essential that vocabulary items should be learnt in the context of a sentence and the sentences must be learnt in situations. This will make the teaching-learning more effective and meaningful. When the teacher follows this principle, the students are able to understand better and they find the learning pleasant and relevant.

### Principle of Accuracy and Correctness

Accuracy refers to the use of right words in right places. The words which impart the exact meaning in the context should alone be used. So the teacher should ensure that the selection of the word is right, use of the word is economical and the expression in impressive.

### Principle of Correlation with Life

The teacher should take all possible efforts to relate the subject matter to life, customs and traditions of the society to which the students belong. This will create interest in students to learn the language to cater to their needs. If the teacher takes pain to follow this principle, this will make teaching more meaningful and learning can be transferred to real life situations. This will facilitate the learning of slow learners to a considerable extent.

### Principle of Balanced Approach

While teaching a foreign language, the teacher should take care of different aspects of language. The four skills of language learning i.e. listening speaking, reading and writing (LSRW) should be equally emphasised. Each aspect has its own importance. If a teacher gives undue importance to one aspect (may be grammar) and ignores other aspects (reading and speaking), his teaching will not yield desired results. Similarly, too much emphasis on written work also does not help much. In this regard Palmer says, "*The principle of proportion does not necessarily imply quality of treatment nor even a fixed standard of ratio; it simply means that all items in the whole range of subjects and aspects must receive an appropriate degree of attention so that the student's knowledge of them may ultimately form a harmonious whole.*"

A good teacher is always in search of good principles and techniques of teaching. He takes initiative to use the innovative methods and techniques in his teaching. He always strives hard to refine his teaching and to make his teaching reach out to all learners. He works for excellence oriented education and his proper application of the verified principles and techniques enables him to give quality based education. In the hands of such teachers even the backward students are able to evince an optimum learning outcome.

## SUMMARY

Teaching is not an easy task as it appears. A teacher has to keep in mind the aims and objectives of teaching the particular language, need and interest of his pupils, the environmental situation in which the teaching learning process takes place etc. Success of a teacher largely depends on good planning and mastery in the subject to be taught.

The principles evolved by the educators enable the teacher to carry on his task of teaching efficiently by showing him the path to be followed and keeping him on the right track. They check him not only from going astray but also optimise the achievement of the teacher in the process of teaching.

The different principles of teaching can work wonders in the hands efficient teachers. The teacher trainees should develop a right insight into these principles and try to put them into use during their teaching practice. The application of these principles will make them better teachers in due course of time.

The maxims explained hitherto are only hints and guidelines for the teachers especially the ones dealing with children at early stage. These are most useful for the teachers teaching the slow learning children who constitute a sizeable portion of student population. The teachers should make use of these maxims in their teaching situations.

There are certain basic principles which are essential for good language teaching. A foreign language teacher must always keep in his mind the basic principles of language teaching to make his teaching more effective. Application of these principles in the instructional process will make the instruction reach out to all the learners.

A good teacher is always in search of good principles and techniques of teaching. He takes initiative to use the innovative methods and techniques in his teaching. He always strives hard to refine his teaching and to make his teaching reach out to all learners. He works for excellence oriented education and his proper application of the verified principles and techniques enables him to give quality based education. In the hands of such teachers even the slow learners are able to evince an optimum learning outcome.

# 4

# Teaching Skills

## TEACHING SKILLS: TAXONOMY OF EDUCATIONAL OBJECTIVES

Often the educational goals described in literature are too vague for any practical purpose. The taxonomy of educational objectives is an attempt to define specific educational objectives. It is a must to evaluate the educational process in terms of realisation of educational objectives.

Generally instructional objectives fall into three domains such as the cognitive domain, the affective domain and the psychomotor domain. Bloom and his associates have formulated the taxonomy of instructional objectives for cognitive and affective domains. R.H. Dave has formulated the taxonomy for psychomotor domain.

### Purposes of Taxonomy or Objectives of Taxonomy

Taxonomy refers to the scientific process of classifying things. The most important purposes of taxonomy are:

1. To establish accuracy of communication regarding objectives of education
2. To reduce the vagueness arising out of loosely defined terms.
3. To ensure more precise communication system in the field of education.
4. To facilitate the understanding of sequence and organisation of human development.
5. To bring uniformity in evaluation

6. To define and evaluate the educational standards of schools.
7. To arrange educational objectives from simple to complex.
8. To facilitate communication among teachers, examiners and other educational workers.
9. To increase the validity and reliability of testing procedures.

**Taxonomy of Educational Objectives**

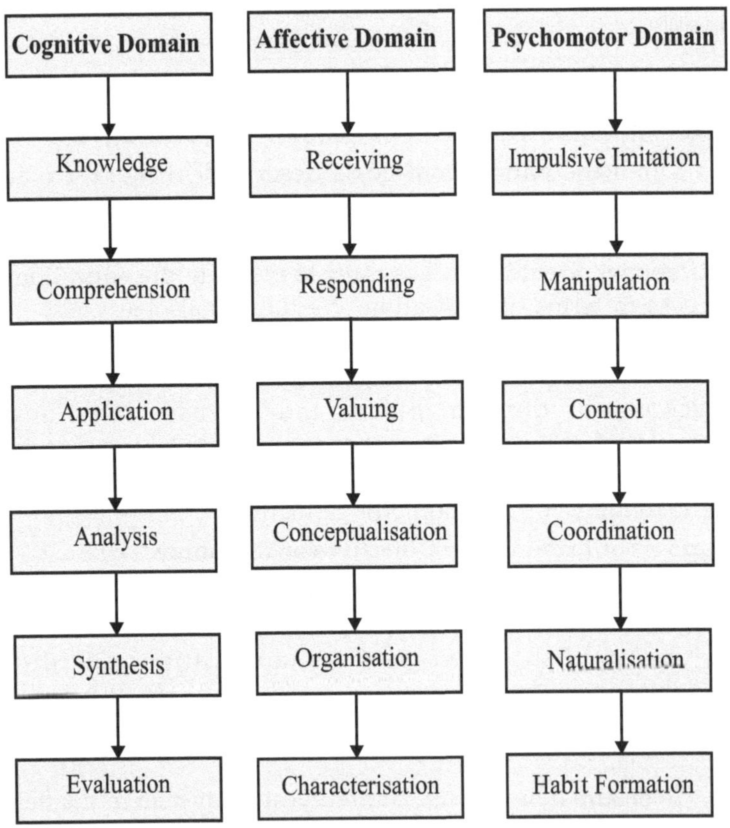


### Cognitive Domain

Bloom and his associates include in this domain those objectives that deal with thinking, knowing and problem solving. The taxonomy contains six classes or categories. They are knowledge, comprehesion, application, analysis, synthesis and evaluation.

**Knowledge**

Knowledge is defined as synonymous with information. It is recalling and recognising facts, information, theory etc. It includes:

**(i) Knowledge of specifics**

It means recalling specific information, terminology and facts. It consists of:

(a) Knowledge of terminology; and
(b) Knowledge of specific facts.

**(ii) Knowledge of ways and means: It includes:**

(a) Knowledge of convention
(b) Knowledge of trends and sequence
(c) Knowledge of criteria
(d) Knowledge of methodology and
(e) Knowledge of classifications and categories

**(iii) Knowledge of universals and abstractions: It includes:**

(a) Knowledge of principles and generalisation; and
(b) Knowledge of theories and structures.

**1. Comprehension**

It means understanding of new knowledge by students. It includes three levels such as:

(i) Translation
(ii) Interpretation
(iii) Extrapolation

**2. Application**

It refers to using ideas, principles and methods in new situations. It includes three levels such as:

(i) Generalisation of principles and ideas;
(ii) Diagnosis of pupil's weakness; and
(iii) Pupils' using terms and laws in their own sentences.

**3. Analysis**

Analysis refers to breaking down of the content into its constituent parts and understanding the relationship and the way they are organised. This objective has also three levels such as:

(i) Analysis of elements
(ii) Analysis of relationship and
(iii) Analysis of organised principles

**4. Synthesis**

Synthesis means putting together parts of elements to form a cogent whole. It includes three levels such as:

(i) Production of unique communication(uniqueness)
(ii) Production of plan or action (originality)
(iii) Reservations of abstract relations (creativity)

**5. Evaluation**

Evaluation means making judgement about the worth. Evaluation is made to assess.

(i) Whether the objectives have been achieved
(ii) Whether the learning experiences created in the class were effective and
(iii) How fairly the teaching objectives have been achieved.

**Affective Domain**

Affective domain is concerned with interest, emotions, attitude and values of students. Bloom has classified the affective objectives into six categories in order to develop the affective domain of the pupils. They are receiving, responding, valuing, conceptualisation, organisation and characterisation.

**1. Receiving or attending**

It refers to sensitivity to the existence of certain phenomenon or stimulus and the learners' willingness to receive it or to attend to it. It has three levels such as:

(i) Awareness of phenomena
(ii) Willingness to receive and
(iii) Controlled or selected attention

**2. Responding**

At this level the learners receive the new knowledge or information under the influence of motivation. It includes three levels such as:

(i) Acquiescence in responding;
(ii) Willingness to respond; and
(iii) Satisfaction in response.

**3. Valuing**

Valuing influences the learners' commitment. They give special importance to what they value. It has three levels such as:

(i) Acceptance of a value
(ii) Preference for values and
(iii) Commitment

**4. Conceptualisation**

Pupils' start forming convictions. They conceptualise the values and decide which to retain.

**5. Organisation**

At this level the learner builds up a value system that includes his behaviour.It includes two levels:

(i) Generalised set; and
(ii) Characterisation

**Psychomotor Domain**

Psychomotor domain includes those objectives which deal with manual and motor skills. The psychomotor objectives are concerned with development of psychomotor skills. Behaviour requiring neuron-manual co-ordination is grouped under this domain. Effort should be made to develop the psychomotor domain of the learners. The categories and the subcategories proposed by R.H.Dave for psychomotor domain are as follows:

(i) Imitation
(ii) Manipulation
(iii) Precision
(iv) Coordination
(v) Naturalisation
(vi) Habit formation

**1. Imitation**

Imitation means copying somebody or something. It includes:

(i) Impulsion-a driving force to learn
(ii) Over repetition

**2. Manipulation**

Manipulation means controlling or using something in a skillful way. It includes:

(i) Following direction
(ii) Selection
(iii) Fixation

**3. Precision**

Precision means being exact or accurate. It requires:

(i) Reproduction; and
(ii) Control.

**4. Co-ordination**

Co-ordination refers to the ability to control movements or making different parts work together in an efficient and organised way. It includes:

(i) sequence; and
(ii) harmony

**5. Naturalisation**

It means showing or doing things in a natural way. It includes:

(i) Automation
(ii) Internalisation

**6. Habit formation**

At this stage, the skill is practised as a habit. It becomes an internalised spontaneous practice where there is a perfect neuron-manual co-ordination

Role or Advantage of Taxonomy in Curriculum and Evaluation

1. Taxonomies help us in analysing and classifying objectives.
2. They give us an idea of how an all round development of the child can be achieved. It rectifies the mistake of over emphasis of one domain in the school programmes.
3. They help us to include all the three domains in the teaching learning process and to develop all the three domains in a balanced way.

4. Taxonomies give guidelines to teachers on how they should report the progress of a child to his parents. Not only the marks obtained in the subject but also an evaluation of his abilities in affective and psychomotor domains should be reported. This makes the evaluation meaningful.

## MICROTEACHING

Micro teaching was developed in Stanford University by Prof. Dwight B. Allow in 1960s. Micro teaching is not a substitute for real teaching. It is only meant for giving intensive training to the teachers under training in different teaching skills. In short, micro teaching is a method of teacher training, not a method of teaching in the classroom.

### Definition

The central idea of this concept is to think clearly and to do something meaningful before you lead as a teacher in the classroom. It is a teacher encounter in a real or simulated situation scaled down in time, in number of pupils and in scope of the content.

### Characteristics of Micro Teaching

- Micro teaching is a teacher training technique.
- It concentrates on one skill at a time.
- The class duration is very short i.e. 5 to 6 minutes.
- The class size is also small, i.e. 5 to 6 fellow trainees.
- It deals with a single concept of subject matter
- It provides for classroom interaction and pin pointed immediate feedback.
- It provides the trainees with teaching techniques employed in the classroom.

### Principles of Micro Teaching

Micro teaching enables teacher trainees to practise a skill by teaching a short lesson to a small number of pupils. Usually, a micro lesson of 5-10 minutes is taught to four or five fellow students. A supervisor using an appraisal guide usually rates the teaching and then discusses it with the teacher trainee. If necessary, the teacher trainee may reteach the lesson to another group of students. This process can be represented.

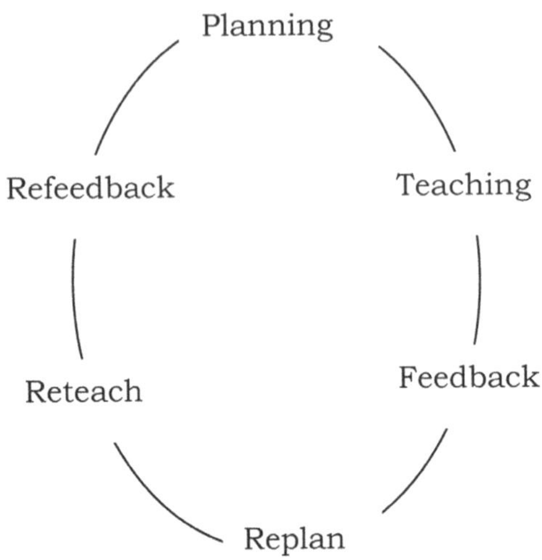


**Micro Teaching Cycle**

**Micro Teaching Skills**

The complex teaching act can be split into component skills. Each skill is simple, well defined and limited. These skills can be identified, practised, evaluated, controlled and acquired through training. There are particular skills which foster teacher pupil interaction. They are:

1. set induction or introduction
2. Explanation
3. Using the blackboard
4. Stimulus variation
5. Reinforcement
6. Skill of questioning
7. Demonstration

***Skill of Set Induction or Introduction***

When you begin a lesson, you have to give a brief introduction. Such introduction influences the students' attitude and secures attention.

**Components of the Skill**

Skill of set induction includes the following components:

(a) Using previous knowledge
(b) Using appropriate device

**Using Previous Knowledge**

The previous knowledge of the students can be tapped out by the following approaches.

1. Refer to or elicit what the students have learnt in previous classes.
2. Refer to or elicit current events which the students might be aware of and
3. Create situations in class and then refer to the relevant knowledge.

**Using Appropriate Device**

A 'device' refers to a technique that is used while introducing a lesson.

The following devices may be used while introducing a lesson

1. Examples
2. Questioning
3. Describing or narrating or illustrating
4. Story telling
5. Dramatisation
6. Audio-visual aids
7. Experimentation or Demonstration

Points to be borne in mind while using appropriate devices

- ❖ Select only suitable device.
- ❖ The devices should be suitable to students' maturity, age, grade, interest, culture and experience
- ❖ The device should be suitable to the nature of the content or subject matter to be taught.

***Skill of Explaining***

Explaining can be defined as an activity to bring about an understanding about a concept, principle etc. It is an activity to fill up a gap in someone's understanding. The skill of explaining aims at making sure that the explanation is understood. The major components in this skill are gaining attention, arousing motivation, establishing rapport and putting the topic in its context. The teacher should state the key concepts clearly and concisely. She can use relevant, simple and clear examples to explain major ideas. She should summarise the main points of the explanation.

**An appraisal guide – skill of set induction**

| | Skill Component | Yes | No | Not seen |
|---|---|---|---|---|
| 1. | Use of previous knowledge | | | |
| | Watching pupils current interest, Comparing and contrasting with the familiar | | | |
| 2. | Appropriateness | | | |
| | Stating the limits and purpose of the task, Suggesting ways to proceed with a task, Using a series of questions | | | |
| 3. | Arouse Interest | | | |
| | Showing enthusiasm, Arousing curiosity, Introducing an element of surprise, Telling a story,Introducing an activity | | | |
| 4. | Effectiveness | | | |
| | Introducing an element or task, Using a series of questions | | | |
| 5. | Gaining attention | | | |
| | Use of voice, gestures and eye contact, use of audio – visual aids, Interaction between teacher and students | | | |

**Components of the Skill of Explaining**

The components of the skill of explaining are:

(a) Using explaining links

(b) Using beginning and concluding statements

(c) Testing student's understanding

**(a) Using explaining links**

Explaining links are the words and phrases which make our explanation clearer.

These links bring continuity in the statements used while teaching. So, appropriate explaining links are to be used to make explanation clear or effective.

List of explaining links:

| | | |
|---|---|---|
| After | but | in spite of |
| As a result | by | next |
| As a result of | due to | so that |
| Because | in order that | such |
| Before | in order to | such that |

**(b) Using beginning and concluding statements**

Before explaining a concept of generalisation, make beginning statement announcing what is to be explained. Such beginning statement prepares students to receive the explanation. Students will become subject oriented and attentive.

After the completion of the explanation, make a concluding statement. Such statements help in strengthening the ideas already explained. This can also be done through summarisation. Hence, both the statements are helpful to students in understanding the content of explanation.

**(c) Testing student's understanding**

The teacher can also ask questions to test student's understanding. It helps to know if the purpose of explaining has been reached. Two or three questions on key points may be asked after the concluding statement.

**An appraisal guide – Skill of Explaining**

| Skill Component | Yes | No | Average | Good | Very Good |
|---|---|---|---|---|---|
| 1. Knowledge of subject | | | | | |
| 2. Clarity of concept | | | | | |
| 3. Fluency of explanation | | | | | |
| 4. Questions to test pupils' understanding | | | | | |
| 5. Planned repetition | | | | | |
| 6. Summarising the main points | | | | | |

***Skill of Using Blackboard***

Blackboard is a visual aid used to write details and to make the ideas clear to the students. Every potential teacher should be proficient in the use of blackboard.

**Components of Blackboard Using Skill**

The blackboard is the visual aid used to write details and make the ideas obvious to a group of students. The blackboard is a friend of the teacher. Using the black board in a classroom is a skill.

**Components of the Skill**

(a) Legibility of handwriting
(b) Neatness in the blackboard
(c) Appropriateness of written work on the blackboard

**(a) Legibility of handwriting**

The handwriting is said to be legible when there is maximum ease in reading it. If the writing is visible and readable, then it is said that handwriting is legible.

The component features of handwriting to be considered for legibility are as follows:

1. Distinct difference between letters
2. Spacing between letters and words
3. Slantness of each letter
4. Size of the letters
5. Size of the upper case (capital) and lower case (small) letters
6. Thickness of the lines

**(b) Neatness in the Blackboard work**

The essential factors for the neatness in the blackboard work are:

(a) Straightness of the lines
(b) Spacing between lines
(c) Avoidance of overwriting
(d) Focusing on the relevant matter

**(c) Appropriateness of work on the blackboard**

The appropriateness of the blackboard work includes:

(a) Continuity in the points
(b) Brevity and simplicity
(c) Drawing attention and focusing

Draw diagrams and figures that are simple, large, clear enough and proportionate in size.

Underline the important points and use coloured chalks for differentiating the different parts of the diagram or figure.

*Skill of Stimulus Variation*

Every teacher has to explain, ask questions, give examples, provide encouraging remarks and motivate students to learn. It is very important to draw and sustain the attention of the students. The skill of stimulus variation can be defined as a deliberate change in the attention drawing behaviour of the teacher in order to secure and sustain students' attention towards the lesson at a high level. This skill is concerned with three major areas of teaching. They are:

1. The manner, voice and teaching style of the teacher.
2. The media and materials used during teaching.
3. The teacher pupil relationship during the class.

**Components of the Skill of Stimulus Variation**

The main components of the skill of stimulus variation are: (a) movement; (b) using gesture; (c) change in the speech pattern; (d) focussing attention; (e) change in interaction style; (f) pausing; (g) oral visual switching.

**(a) Moving in the classroom**

Teacher's movements in the classroom carry wide significance in securing and sustaining students' attention. So teachers should make well-planned meaningful movements. They should move in the class during the following situations:

- To explain a picture hung on the wall;
- To write important formulae on the blackboard; and
- To check whether the students are noting the diagram drawn on the blackboard.

**(b) Using gestures**

The oral message combined with gestural ones is more effective in conveying meaning than an oral message used singly. Gestures will make presentation more expressive, dynamic and also help in drawing student's attention.

**(c) Change in speech pattern**

To express emotions or feelings, the teacher can modulate his voice. This sudden variation in this stimulus will attract the students. It will also make the students attend to the idea being told to them.

**(d) Focussing attention**

This component involves the use of such behaviours that direct or focus students' attention to a particular point which the students have to notice or observe. Such behaviours include three types of focusing.

**Verbal Focusing**

Direct or focus student's attention to significant points by using statements such as 'Listen carefully to this', 'Now this is important'. This is a point worth noting etc.

**Gestural Focusing**

This involves focusing or directing students' attention to particular points in teaching by using mainly hand movement. Eg; Point with a pointer some places on a map.

**Verbal and Gestural Focusing**

Focus students attention both by pointing to a figure and saying verbally like 'look at this figure'.

**(e) Change in interaction styles**

When two or more persons communicate with each other orally, there is said to be oral interaction between them. In a class there are three types of interaction styles.

**1. Teacher group interaction**

Ask questions to the whole class and elicit responses to the same question individually from any students.

**2. Teacher student interaction**

Ask an individual student a question, receive an answer and follow it up with series of questions to the same student, when you want to probe into the issue more deeply.

**3. Student-student interaction**

Ask a question and without commenting redirect the question by pointing to another student. Try to involve many students in a dialogue without doing direct discussion.

**(f) Pausing**

Pausing means introducing silence during talk. In order to sustain student's attention introduce certain pauses during teaching.

Teachers can use pause during the following occasions:

- ❖ Use the pause after each sentence or between successive sentences.
- ❖ Use pause for a few seconds immediately after asking a question
- ❖ Use pause occasionally to give students an opportunity to formulate ideas.

**Oral-visual switching**

The teacher may provide information through oral medium or through visual medium. Sometimes he may be doing both simultaneously i.e., information through oral-visual media. If a teacher is talking continuously, students will feel bored. Hence teacher has to change these situations. Such changes are:

Oral ⇌ Oral - Visual

Oral ⇌ Visual

Visual ⇌ Oral - Visual

An appraisal guide – Stimulus variation

| Skill Component | 1 | 2 | 3 | 4 | 5 | 6 | 7 | 8 | 9 | 10 |
|---|---|---|---|---|---|---|---|---|---|---|
| 1. Teacher movement | | | | | | | | | | |
| 2. Teacher gestures | | | | | | | | | | |
| 3. Change in speech pattern | | | | | | | | | | |
| 4. Change in sensory focus | | | | | | | | | | |
| 5. Verbal pupil pattern | | | | | | | | | | |
| 6. Pupil activity | | | | | | | | | | |

*Skill of Reinforcement*

Skill of reinforcement is very important in teaching learning process:

1. To attract and retain the attention of the class.
2. To encourage the pupils to strive harder
3. To improve classroom discipline and modify destructive behaviour
4. To increase pupils' confidence

Major components

The following are the major components of the reinforcement skill.

| | | |
|---|---|---|
| Verbal reinforcement | – | comments like "Good" well done, etc. |
| Gestural reinforcement | – | Facial expressions e.g. a smile |
| Proximity reinforcement | – | Teacher moving nearer to the student |
| Contact reinforcement | – | Patting the head, back etc |
| Activity reinforcement | – | Teacher gives the pupils a task they prefer as reinforcement e.g. a project etc. |
| Token reinforcement | – | The teacher awards marks, merit cards, writing comments like good. |

**An appraisal guide – Reinforcement skill**

| Components | Tallies |
|---|---|
| 1. Verbal reinforcement | |
| 2. Gestural reinforcement | |
| 3. Proximity reinforcement | |
| 4. Contact reinforcement | |
| 5. Activity reinforcement | |
| 6. Token reinforcement | |

Reinforcement skill can increase students' involvement in their lessons in a number of ways. Skill of reinforcement is very essential to ensure effective teaching learning process.

*Skill of Questioning*

It refers to the ability to frame, different types of questions so as to suit the level and requirement. Teacher must be able to frame the following types of questions.

1. **Low level question:** These questions require student's recall. The response requires memorisation on the put of the students.
2. **High level question:** These questions require a degree of intellectual processing on the part of the students i.e. comprehension, application, analogy, synthesis and valuation
3. **Description questions:** These questions require the students to describe a process or product or an event. It promotes students' involvement.

4. **Comparison questions:** These questions require the students to look at two or more objects or statements and to identify similarities and differences
5. **Convergent questions:** These are the questions which have one answer. These are questions of fact or recall
6. **Divergent questions:** These are the questions which have different answers. They require creative thinking
7. **Redirection questions:** These questions involve large number of students. It creates high level of interaction.
8. **Prompting:** Prompting is required when a student is not able to respond to a question. Prompting has two components such as basic question and advance question.

**An Appraisal Guide – Skill of Questioning**

| **Basic Questioning** | **Very Good** | **Good** | **Average** | **Poor** | **Very Poor** |
|---|---|---|---|---|---|
| Phrasing – Clarity and brevity | | | | | |
| Focussing | | | | | |
| Direction | | | | | |
| Distribution – Whole class | | | | | |
| Specific Pupils | | | | | |
| Pausing | | | | | |
| Prompting | | | | | |
| Rephrase | | | | | |
| Simpler questions | | | | | |
| **Advance Questioning** | | | | | |
| Varying the level | | | | | |
| Recalling | | | | | |
| Comprehension | | | | | |
| Application | | | | | |
| Analysis | | | | | |
| Synthesis | | | | | |
| Evaluation | | | | | |
| Probing | | | | | |
| Clarification | | | | | |
| Support | | | | | |
| Consensus | | | | | |
| Examples | | | | | |
| Pausing | | | | | |

*Skill of Demonstration*

Skill of demonstration is the most required skill to teach science subjects. Demonstration facilitates observation of process and acquisition of knowledge. While demonstrating, teacher poses questions to draw the attention of the students. Hence this skill is called skill of lecturing and demonstration.

**Components of Skill of Demonstration**

There are eight components in this skill. They are: *(i)* clear objective; *(ii)* usage of suitable apparatus; *(iii)* arrangement of apparatus; *(iv)* handling of apparatus; *(v)* visibility; *(vi)* students' participation; *(vii)* usage of blackboard; and *(viii)* skill of explanation.

**Clear objective:** The objectives and aims of the demonstration must be specified clearly. The process is also mentioned clearly.

**Usage of suitable apparatus:** Suitable apparatus for demonstration must be collected earlier. Materials required for demonstration must be kept on the demonstration table.

**Arrangement of apparatus:** Instruments required for demonstration must be kept in their proper places. Materials to be taken from the right side can be kept at right side and vice versa.

**Handling of apparatus:** Teacher must possess the skill to handle the apparatus properly and safely. Chemicals must be handled safety. Perfect handling of apparatus is a must.

**Visibility:** The demonstration table must be visible to all the students' view. To ensure visibility big apparatus can be used. Table of reasonable height may be used. Semi circle seat arrangement is ideal. Room should have proper ventilation and lighting arrangement.

**Students' participation:** During demonstration students' participation must be ensured. Questions can be asked to elicit response. Students can be encouraged to explain important points.

**Usage of black board:** Black board must be effectively used for writing, drawing and deriving conclusions.

**Ability to explain:** Effective explanation is a must to make the demonstration understandable to students. Doing the demonstration without corresponding explanation will be of no use.

**An Appraisal Guide – Skill of Demonstration**

| Components | Very Good | Good | Average | Poor | Very Poor |
|---|---|---|---|---|---|
| 1. Clear Objectives | | | | | |
| 2. Suitable apparatus | | | | | |
| 3. Arrangement of apparatus | | | | | |
| 4. Handling of apparatus | | | | | |
| 5. Visibility | | | | | |
| 6. Students participation | | | | | |
| 7. Black board usage | | | | | |
| 8. Explanation | | | | | |

**Link Practice or Link Lesson**

In our involvement with the micro teaching programme we should not lose sight of the main issue which is to train teacher trainees to do full class teaching successfully making use of a variety of skills. So link practice provides a bridge between micro teaching and full class teaching or macro teaching. It is done by.

1. Increasing the class size to about 15 pupils;
2. Increasing the length of the lesson to about 20-30 minutes; and
3. Integrating the skills practised in micro teaching.

The trainee also has to teach a number of lessons as a unit of work. Finally, after micro teaching and link practice, the trainee moves to full class teaching. He thus moves from "Shallow – end" to the 'deep-end'.

| Characteristics | Micro Lesson | Link Lesson | Macro Lesson |
|---|---|---|---|
| (i) Time limit for practising skills | 5 minutes | 20 minute generally | 45 minutes |
| (ii) Class size | 5 or 6 peer group members | 20 school students | 40 school students |
| (iii) Number of skills | One | More than one | Several depending on size of unit |
| (iv) content size | One single concept small | A part of a unit | A whole unit |

## OBSERVATION

Observation means the act of watching for a period of time to learn more about something. Observation provides direct knowledge of behaviour. It is useful for teachers to understand the nature of students in terms of attention, participation, cooperation, study habits, self control etc.

### Stages of Observation

There are four stages of observation. They are: *(i)* perception; *(ii)* recording of what is observed; *(iii)* classification and analysis of behaviour; and *(iv)* generalisation.

### Types of Observation

Observation may be of different types such as direct and indirect, natural and artificial scheduled and unscheduled and participant and non-participant. In natural observation, observation is done in natural setting. In artificial observation, it is done in simulated or controlled setting.

### Measures to Improve Observation

There are certain measures to improve observation. Some of them are as follows:

**1. Use of mechanical devices**

Use of mechanical devices like movie camera, tap recorder, one way see through glass will improve the reliability of observation. Here there is no place for personal bias and prejudice.

**2. Defining objectives**

Defining objectives in specific and concrete terms will improve observation. A detailed analysis of behavioural characteristics to be observed should be made.

**3. Schedule**

Schedule refers to the time and hour of observation. It should be followed honestly. A detailed schedule in the forms of questions or statements should be prepared in advance to note down the observation.

**4. Training**

Training enhances observation skill. It is not an activity. It is a systematic and scientific method which requires skill and proper training.

**5. Practice**

Practice gives perfection and improves observation skill. Observation becomes more reliable when the investigator provides quantitative description of data. This requires more practice.

**Observing a Lesson**

1. Observer should go round the class. He should interact with students for clarifying purpose.
2. Observation should be noted in the lesson plan itself
3. Observers should provide feedback
4. A team of observers can observe and share the observation among themselves and provide feedback.
5. Class teacher should give the observers charts or name list or tags.

## DEMONSTRATION LESSON

It is a model lesson taken by the teacher educator or the guide teacher for the understanding and emulation of teacher trainees. The trainees should observe the demonstration lesson carefully. They shall observe:

- how the teacher educator motivates the students;
- how he uses the blackboard;
- how he uses models and teaching aids;
- how he presents the lesson and proceeds;

The teacher educator taking the model lesson should:

- make use of proper body language
- use voice modulation, gestures, facial expression etc
- ask small questions to make formative evaluation

- encourage students by saying 'good' 'yes' 'come on' etc.
- prepare the lesson in advance
- use the latest teaching method
- use appropriate teaching aids

## TEACHER EDUCATOR

A teacher who teaches student teachers at B.Ed., and M.Ed., levels is known as teacher educator. A teacher educator must possess the following competencies to make the teaching learning process more effective.

**1. Proficiency in language**

The teacher educator must be proficient in language. He should be able to use freely the vocabulary and structures. His pronunciation must be good. He must be able to write in accepted style. He must be able to correct the reports and letters written by students.

**2. Knowledge of Linguistics**

The teacher educator must know the semantics and syntactic. He must know the linguistic facts of the language so that he can understand the problems the students may be likely to have. He must know the similarities and dissimilarities between English and the mother tongue.

**3. Ability to use different teaching techniques**

The teacher must be able to use audio-lingual methods and techniques. He must be familiar with the modern theory and practice in testing of language aptitude, achievement and proficiency.

### Role of the English Teacher

A teacher is a successful guide. To be a successful man-maker, he should posses the following qualities: *(i)* objectivity; *(ii)* deep knowledge of the subject; *(iii)* application of theory; *(iv)* well informed; *(v)* widely travelled; *(vi)* a good communicator; *(vii)* skill in the use of technological aid; *(viii)* an interpreter of various experiences.

### Guide Teacher

Guide teacher is a teacher who guides the student teachers during teaching practice.

An efficient guide teacher should have the following qualities:

- ❖ He should have deep insight into the nature and needs of pupils and should be able to deal with them in spirit of friendly rapport.
- ❖ He should be sensitive to students' feelings and problems.
- ❖ He should be receptive and listen most of the time to what his clients have to say
- ❖ He should be professionally trained in counselling skills.
- ❖ He should be thorough with information and knowledge needed to give effective guidance.
- ❖ He should be highly objective in approach.
- ❖ He should help his clients to achieve self adjustment and self-direction.
- ❖ Optimism and sympathy should govern all his interactions with clients.
- ❖ He should act as source of moral.
- ❖ He must be convinced that the project is within the capacity of the pupil, is easy and can be completed.
- ❖ He should assist the project in advance without deeply involving himself in it.
- ❖ He should insure that the project selected has definite educational values.

**Peer Group**

Peer means one who is equal in rank, merit, age, emotion, thinking, moral etc. Peer group is a group having members of same age group/class. Individuality of the group members is lost in the group. The sense of identity with the group is dominant. The type of behaviour found in the group in called group behaviour.

**Characteristics of Group Behaviour**

The following are the characteristics of group behaviour:

1. Common goals, interests and ideas
2. Similar behaviour and attitude
3. Control of the group

4. Mutual obligation
5. Sense of belongingness and oneness
6. Influence of the group characteristics
7. Psychological relationship between members

**Feedback**

Feed back is an advice or criticism or information about how good something was or someone's action was. Feedback is provided on the skill under practice by the teacher educator or by the guide or by the peer. It enables the trainee to replay his lesson on the basis of the feedback. It enables the trainees to modify their approach and to reteach well. Feedback plays an instrumental role in micro teaching in perfection and refinement of teaching skills.

**Characteristics of Good English Teacher**

The following are the characteristics of a good English teacher:

1. He should have an indepth knowledge of English language with adequate skill in listening, speaking, reading and writing.
2. He should know the objective of teaching English as a second language
3. He should have an adequate insight into the various forms of English literature prose, poetry, drama, stories, novels etc
4. He should evince interest and favourable attitude towards teaching English.
5. He should be able to write the objectives of teaching various forms of English in behavioural terms.
6. He should have an insight into the various methods, techniques, devices and maxims of teaching English.
7. He should be able to diagnose the learning difficulties and prepare remedial instruction to overcome those difficulties.
8. He should be able to differentiate between English language teaching and English literature teaching at various stages.
9. He should possess moral character and set himself as a good model for the students.

10. He should use a variety of techniques to avoid monotony and make the class lively.
11. He must be intellectual, impartial, devoted and dedicated with mastery over skills and subject matter.

## MACROTEACHING

Macro teaching is the normal classroom teaching in real situation. The topic, the size of the class and the duration of the period are usually large. There is focus on development of all skills. More than one objective are achieved with the help of macro lesson plan. The cognitive and affective learning objectives can be achieved by the macro lesson. Macro lessons are prepared and practised in the traditional teaching practices.

### Planning for Instruction

Planning for instruction means that the teacher should think over lesson in advance so as to ensure an effective teaching learning process. Planning is of great importance in the teaching – learning process. Unless the teacher plans well, he won't be able to do justice in the class. In the same way, the learner has also to plan things. Then only he can learn better and can use the learnt material in a good way. We know that teaching is organised in three phases i.e. Pre active, interactive and post active. Before entering the class-room whatever activities a teacher plans, may be put in pre-active phase of teaching. Lesson planning is virtually the pre-active phase of teaching.

"A Lesson plan", in the words of Lester. B.Stands, *"is actually a plan of action. It, therefore, includes the working philosophy of the teacher, his knowledge of philosophy, his information about and understanding of his pupils, his comprehension of the objectives of education his knowledge of the material to be taught and his ability to utilize effective methods".*

### Planning a Lesson

There are different stages of planning, They are: *(i)* Pre-teaching planning; *(ii)* Planning during teaching; and *(iii)* Post teaching planning.

**(i) Pre-teaching planning**

Before teaching a lesson to some class the teacher prepares notes at home. Then he plans over everything of the lesson i.e. what he is going to present, how he is going to present, what techniques he is going to use, which audio-visual aids he is going to make use of etc.

**(ii) Planning during teaching**

While teaching in the class, the teacher is to plan the blackboard writing in systematic way, plan the activities of the students etc. The teacher also knows before hand what types of mistakes will be committed by the students and he thinks of their solution.

**(iii) Post - teaching planning:**

It is a stage when the teacher has finished the class-room teaching. At this stage, he is to see how far he has been successful in teaching. He brings to his mind the good and bad points of his teaching. He plans about the correction of written work enlisting the errors of the students, preparation of exercises for improvements etc.

**Characteristics of a Good lesson Plan**

A good lesson plan is like a cloth. From the lesson plan, we can guess somewhat about the teacher, his method of teaching provided the lesson plan is made by the teacher himself.

**A good lesson plan has the following characteristics**

1. General and specific aims of teaching a lesson are revealed in it.
2. From the lesson plan, we at once come to know about the different audio-visual aids which are going to be used in the teaching.
3. It shows the activities done by the teacher and the students in the class room.
4. It tells us about the general procedure adopted by the teacher for teaching. The method of handling the language material is also revealed.
5. There is mention of assignment or home work which is to be given to the students.

6. From the lesson plan we come to know the reference books referred by the teacher while preparing it. In a good lesson plan there is always a mention of it.

**Advantages of Planning a Lesson**

1. It keeps the teacher to be systematic and orderly in the treatment of the subject-matter. He proceeds on well thought of and definite lines and does not indulge in haphazard and thoughtless teaching.
2. The teacher sets forth with some definite aims in view and is conscious of the interest, attitude, etc., that he is to develop in the students through certain activities or some other means.
3. Planning a lesson gives confidence and self-reliance to the teacher, which is of great value for successful teaching.
4. It saves time in the sense that the students get a better understanding of the subject and form some desirable attitudes and habits that would otherwise have been impossible in the same period.
5. It encourages the continuity in the teaching process.

## TEACHING OF PROSE

Prose is a meaningful unit with the best words in the best order. Prose is for knowledge, information and language. Appreciation of prose involves comprehending the phrase, structures, allusion and images in the text besides the central concept or the theme.

**Characteristics of Prose**

1. Prose consists of philosophical ideas, social problems, historical description of events, geographical concepts etc.
2. Prose is the most important aspects of literature. Thoughts on a topic, story, drama novels, autobiography and biography, narration and explanation of concepts, theories and principles are the major aspects of prose.
3. Prose develops listening, reading, speaking and writing skills.
4. The purpose of literature is best served by prose.
5. Prose develops the expressional and interpretative ability of students.

6. Prose develops cognitive and affective aspects of students.
7. Prose is the best way of preserving human knowledge, experiences, imagination etc. and transmitting them to new generations.

**General Objectives of Teaching Prose**

The following are the general objectives of teaching prose:

1. To enable the students to understand the passage or the lesson.
2. To develop the imaginative power of the students.
3. To enable the students to enjoy reading English literature.
4. To enrich the students' active and passive vocabulary.
5. To enable the students to read the passage with correct pronunciations, intonation, pause and articulation of voice.
6. To prepare the students for world citizenship.

**Various Forms of Prose**

There are various forms of prose. They are essay, novel, story, and play or drama.

**Essay**

It is short piece of writing on a particular topic. Essay may be personal, philosophical, historical or critical. They may be long or short in size. It depends on the grade level.

**Novel**

It is a story long enough to make a book in which all characters are imaginary. Originally it meant a fresh story. Now it means a long story in prose. It differs from a story in verse.

**Story**

It is an account of past events or of how something has developed. It shares the visual constituents and setting. Stories are short in scope, size and content.

**Play**

It is a piece of writing performed by the actors in the theatre. A play has a plot, character, dialogue and setting, it is meant to be performed in public, not to be read in private.

**Other Forms**

There are some other forms of prose. They are biography, autobiography, travelogue, paragraph, composition etc.

**Procedure for Teaching Prose Lesson**

The following procedure should be followed by a teacher in teaching prose:

1. Motivation or introduction
2. Introduction of new grammatical structures
3. Introduction of new vocabulary
4. Model reading by teacher
5. Silent reading by the pupils
6. Testing comprehension
7. Word study or explaining difficult words
8. Reading aloud by the pupils
9. Assignment oral or written

**1. Motivation or introduction**

This is the first step. Teacher has to motivate the students to ensure learning readiness. This is common to all subjects. Audio visual aids can be used for this purpose. If it is an on-going lesson, a few questions can be asked to recall the previous knowledge of the students.

**2. New grammatical structure:**

Now a days we follow structural approach. So teaching new structure is given preference. Structures are graded on the principle utility, teachability and suitability to the class. Structures are introduced by creating visual or verbal situation. Teacher should provide oral drill and practice of the structures.

**3. New vocabulary**

There are two types of vocabulary. i.e. active vocabulary and passive vocabulary. Teacher should give the meaning of new words and explain the usage. Students should know the meaning. They should be taught to use the new words in their sentences.

**4. Model Reading by the teacher**

Teacher should read the lesson first. It is model reading. Students keep the book closed and listen to teacher's reading.

The teacher should read the lesson observing, pause, stress, rhythm and intonation correctly. Students should listen carefully. Second reading is done with pupils keeping open their readers. This provides required practice in aural comprehension.

5. **Explaining difficult words**

The teacher reads the passage twice. Students may come across difficult words. Such words should be explained thoroughly by the teacher.

6. **Silent reading by pupils**

Each student reads silently and comprehends at his own pace. Teacher fixes time limit to develop speed in reading. Teacher corrects habits like finger movement and lip movement.

7. **Testing comprehension**

Students complete reading. Then teacher asks questions to test their level of understanding. First, he asks simple yes or no or objective type questions. Then he goes for short answer type, inference type and essay type questions. If the response is not satisfactory, he can drill up the passage.

8. **Reading aloud by pupils**

This is necessary to develop correct reading habits. It helps in correcting errors in pause, stress and intonation. Group reading is good for lower classes. Individual reading is good for higher classes.

9. **Assignment oral or written**

Assignment at the end is a must. It enables the students to remember the meaning of the words and use them in own sentences. It helps the students consolidate the knowledge acquired or the concept learnt.

**Teaching of Poetry**

Poetry is musical and metrical form of language. Poetry is a thing of beauty, of form of thought and of emotion. It is intimately woven with nature and life. It appeals to heart. Wordsworth says, *"Poetry is the spontaneous overflow of powerful feelings". According to Coleridge, "poetry is the best words in the best order".*

### Advantages of Teaching Poetry

- Poetry has tremendous appeal for children. It is the best way of developing their love for language. It develops aesthetic and intuitive sense in children.
- Poetry refines our emotions. Prose is like walking; Poetry is like dancing.
- Poetry is memorable because of its rhyme and rhythm.
- Poetry imparts pleasure to students. It lays the foundation for appreciation.
- Poetry introduces variety in English course. It is a good antidote against boredom.

### General Objectives of Teaching Poetry

The following are the general objectives of teaching poetry:

1. To enable students to appreciate beauty, rhyme and style of the poem.
2. To enable pupils to read aloud the poem with proper rhythm and intonation.
3. To enable students to enjoy recitation, thought and imagination involved in the poem.
4. To develop the aesthetic sense and create love for English literature in them.

### Methods of Teaching Poetry

Methods of teaching poetry include:

1. Lecture method
2. Question answer method
3. Review method
4. Meaning and understanding method

### Techniques of Teaching Poetry

Techniques of teaching poetry include the following:

1. Question-Answer technique
2. Model reading
3. Explanation technique
4. Parallel quotation technique
5. Narration technique

## Procedure of Teaching Poetry

The procedure includes preparation, objectives, teaching aids, previous knowledge.

Introduction

Presentation

Presenting the gist of the poem

Model reading by the teacher

Pronunciation drill

Model reading II by the teacher

Explaining difficult words and phrases

Model reading III by the teacher

Comprehension questions

Appreciation Questions

Chorus recitation

Assignment

## Introduction

According to Thompson and Watt poems can be introduced by: *(i)* reading a parallel poem; *(ii)* giving the gist of the poem; *(iii)* by giving the life sketch, style and the characteristics of the poet.

A good poem is a complete whole. So poetry must be taught as one unit. It should not be taught in parts.

## Presenting the Gist of the Poem

Teacher should give the gist of the poem. It will enable the students to understand the theme in a better way.

## Model Reading I by the Teacher

Teacher recites the poem. Students listen with book closed. This helps the students to follow the musical tone. The model reading helps the students to feel the poem in its totality.

## Pronunciation Drill

Teacher pronounces the difficult words. Students repeat after him, drill is provided till they pronounce the words correctly.

### Model Reading II

Teacher gives the second reading. Students listen with book open. Students keenly observe the modulation of the teacher.

### Meaning of Difficult Words or Phrases

Words affecting comprehension should be explained by the teacher. Use of particular word or phrase or epithet and its significance can be highlighted. Figures of speech can also be highlighted.

### Model Reading III

Third reading is given for greater effect. Imitation reading is done by the pupils. Pupils may be asked to recite with proper rhyme, rhythm and intonation.

### Comprehension Questions

Simple questions may be posed to assess the understanding of the students.

### Appreciation Questions

These questions are posed to assess the students' appreciation of beauty of images and the beauty of style and language.

### Chorus Recitation

It is essential at lower classes. This enables the students to practise rhyme, rhythm and intonation. It helps the pupils to overcome their shyness. It develops eloquence and fluency.

### Assignment

Assignment is not much emphasised in teaching poetry. Teacher may ask the pupils to write down the rhyming words. He can ask them to memorise the poem.

### Difference Between Teaching of Prose and Teaching of Poetry

| | Teaching of Prose | Teaching of Poetry |
|---|---|---|
| 1. | Prose lesson is taught for development of language aspects. | Poem is taught for pleasure and enjoyment. |
| 2. | Grammar and structures are dealt with in detail. | Grammar and structures are not dealt with. |
| 3. | New words are explained and the usages are highlighted. | Just meaning is given to facilitate understanding. |

*(Contd...)*

| Teaching of Prose | Teaching of Poetry |
|---|---|
| 4. Prose lesson is taught in part. | Poem is taught as a whole. |
| 5. Not much emphasis on model reading. | More emphasis is on model reading. |
| 6. There is greater need for assignment. | There is limited scope for assignment. |
| 7. Prose is taught for information or knowledge. | Poem is taught for appreciation and pleasure. |
| 8. It is taught for linguistic effect. | It is taught for musical effect. |
| 9. Prose teaching appeals to mind or reason. i.e. Development cognition domain. | Poetry teaching appeals to emotion or feeling i.e. Development of affective domain. |

### Poetic Forms

The following are the various poetic forms in English:

| Personal or Subjective Poetry | Impersonal or Objective Poetry |
|---|---|
| The lyrics | Ballad |
| The ode | Epic |
| The elegy | Metrical Romance |
| Sonnet | Dramatic Monologue |

### Poetic Diction

*(i)* Feet of two syllable the limbic and the trochaic; *(ii)* Feet of three syllable anapaestic dactylic and amphibrachic; *(iii)* Metre; *(iv)* Stanza; *(v)* Rime; *(vi)* Alliteration; *(vii)* Blank verse; *(viii)* Figures of speech.

1. Poetic diction is figurative and allusive.
2. Poetic diction is passionate and beautiful.
3. Poetic diction is a natural magic of expression.
4. Poetic diction is felicity of phrasing

## TEACHING OF COMPOSITION

Composition is a short text written as school exercise. Composition is an advanced stage of learning to write on some topics of interest in a systematic way.

**Principles of Teaching Composition**

| | |
|---|---|
| 1. Principle of selection | – Selection should be made on the basis of interest and experience. |
| 2. Principle of gradation | – Composition should be graded according to age and class level. |
| 3. Principle of oral practice | – Oral practice should precede written composition. |
| 4. Principle of sequence | – Subject matter should be arranged in logical sequence. |
| 5. Principle of timely correction | – Written works of students should be corrected within reasonable time. |

**Types of Composition**

There are two types of composition. They are: *(i)* Oral composition; *(ii)* Written composition.

**Oral Composition**

Oral composition should precede written composition. Oral composition includes:

1. Asking students to produce the sentence of the teacher
2. Teacher asking about some object or activity
3. Asking students to describe a picture or event
4. Conversation practice
5. Dialogue practice
6. Dramatisation practice

**Guided Composition**

Here the students are provided with necessary vocabulary and structures required for writing. Teacher guides the students how to write with the given vocabulary and structures. The teacher corrects the writings of the students and guides again if necessary.

**Free Composition**

Here students are encouraged to write on their own. They use the vocabulary and structures of their own to express their own ideas. This is called free composition. It is creative and original in nature.

**Types of Free Composition**

The various types of free compositions are: *(i)* Paragraph writing; *(ii)* Paraphrasing; *(iii)* Essay writing; *(iv)* descriptive writing.

## AIMS OFTEACHING INTENSIVE READER

The following are the aims of teaching reader:

- To comprehend the lesson thoroughly.
- To master the structures and vocabulary in the given text
- To acquire mastery over the written language.
- To develop oral discussions.
- To know the meaning of difficult words, phrases and ideas.
- To learn new words in plenty
- To understand grammatical structures
- To develop familiarity with the contexts.
- To obtain the habit of reading

### Aims of Teaching Extensive Reader

Extensive reader is taught for the following reasons.

- To create an interest in reading for pleasure
- To increase their reading speed
- To develop desirable silent reading skills
- To learn to guess the meanings of some words from the context in which they have been used
- To grasp the central idea of the passage read
- To follow the sequence of ideas, & events etc in the passage

## CRITERIA FOR SELECTION OF A READER

Selection of a Reader or textbook is based on many important factors. We should consider the knowledge of the learners, their background, their aptitude, attitude and their entry behaviour. The following are the vital criteria for selection of a reader.

1. **Subject matter**: The subject matter should be simple and interesting. It must be within the knowledge and experience level of the students. Complicated, confusing and controversial themes should be avoided.
2. **Language**: The language should be simple and comprehensive. It must be appropriate to the level of learners. The ratio of new words and known words should be carefully maintained.

3. **Illustration**: Textbooks should have appealing illustrations like pictures, diagrams, graphs, tables etc which will facilitate better understanding and longer retention.
4. **Skills and activities**: The reader should have sufficient exercises, assignments and projects to provide for activities and to improve their skills. Language Reader should have adequate exercises for pronunciation, stress, pause, intonation etc.
5. **Guidance to the teacher**: The text book should provide guidance to the teachers to do their job in a better way. They should find the textbook as a handy tool for effective teaching.
6. **Glossary**: A glossary of new words must be given at the end of each lesson. It is very useful for students' understanding. It should provide for strengthening the word power of the students.

Teaching English Grammar

## DEFINITION OF GRAMMAR

Grammar is the theory of language and the study of organisation of words into sentences. Plato and his pupil Aristotle were the first to take up this subject seriously. Sweet has defined grammar as, *"the practical analysis of a language and its anatomy" According to Champman, "Grammar is a study of language by specialists, made in order to establish the rules and principles which are followed more or less unconsciously or instinctively by the native speakers"* Grammar has three different meanings.

### Three meanings of grammar

Grammar has three different meanings:

1. It is the set of formal patterns in which the words of a language are arranged in order to convey larger meanings.
2. It is the branch of linguistic science which is concerned with the description, analysis and formalisation of formal language patterns
3. It is linguistic etiquette.

## Objectives of Teaching Grammar

Objectives of teaching grammar include:

1. To develop students' insight into the structures of English language.
2. To enable the students to assimilate the correct English language and grammar.
3. To teach grammar as a rule-governed behaviour.
4. To develop their mental abilities of reasoning and correct observation.
5. To develop a scientific attitude in pupils about the language.

## Types of Grammar

There are five types of grammar. They are: *(i)* prescriptive or formal grammar; *(ii)* descriptive or functional grammar; *(iii)* structural grammar; *(iv)* transformational generative grammar; and *(v)* communicative grammar.

### 1. Prescriptive grammar

It is also called formal or theoretical grammar. It is the old traditional grammar. In it the main emphasis is on rules and forms. It prescribes its norms upon the language users. It is traditional in approach. It does not allow changes in language, whereas change in rules is a must.

### 2. Descriptive or functional grammar

Its main emphasis is on the functional side of the language. It describes the behaviour of the language. It changes along with the change in language.

### 3. Structural grammar

C.C. Fries, an American Linguist, founded this type of grammar. The grammar is taught on the basis of structure of sentences. The structural grammarians prefer to study the grammatical forms (structures) of the language before considering their lexical meaning.

### 4. Transformational – Generative Grammar

Its emphasis is laid upon the sentences. The grammarians of this school recognise that there are sentences basic to the language, sentences from which all others are derived. The approach here is characterised by abstraction. The components of this sort of grammar are phonological, syntactic and semantic.

**5. Communicative grammar:**

This type of grammar is functional and task-based. The grammarians of this school focus their attention on meaning rather than on form of expressions. In the divergent situations they describe the communicative value and significance of each utterance or expression. Most of these grammarians prefer fluency in the use of language to accuracy.

**Principles of Teaching Grammar**

The following principles should be kept in mind while teaching grammar:

1. In the beginning stages, a separate grammar book is not needed. Pupils should absorb the grammatical items in the reader unconsciously.
2. Grammar should not be begun on abstract lines.
3. Grammar principles should begin with language. It must correlate speech with reading.
4. Grammar and usage should be taught simultaneously with their own examples.
5. Grammar should be taught as an intellectual exercise. The main aim is to make the pupils skilful users of the language.
6. Grammar knowledge should enable the pupils to build their own structures.

**Four Stages of Grammar Learning**

The following are the four stages of grammar learning.

1. **Perception:** In this stage, the pupils perceive the form and the meaning of the grammatical items either in speech or writing or in both.
2. **Understanding:** In this stage, the learners understand what the grammatical item looks like and what it means and how it sounds and functions.
3. **Absorption:** At this stage, learners do a series of varied exercises based on the grammatical item. They absorb the rule, usage and function.

4. **Demonstration:** In this stage, test is administered and the learners demonstrate how well they have learnt the grammar items.

**Methods of Teaching Grammar**

There are various methods of teaching grammar. They are:

*(i)* The traditional method; *(ii)* the informal method; *(iii)* the reference and correlation method; and *(iv)* the inductive – deductive method.

**(i) The traditional method**

The teacher tells a definition or explains the rule to the students. Then he gives examples and exercises. For example, teacher says, "A noun is the name of a person or place or thing". Then he gives many examples for noun. After that, he refers to the exercise in the textbook and asks the pupils to point out the noun in it. The same procedure is followed for teaching other parts of speech and other grammatic items such as synthesis, analysis and transformation. Pupils commit rules to memory and solve the exercises in the reader.

**Limitations**

This method suffers from the following limitations: (a) It emphasis cramming; (b) It is against the educational maxims, "proceed from simple to complex" and "proceed from known to unknown"; (c) Students find it least interesting.

**(ii) The informal method**

This method emphasises teaching grammar not by rules but by usages. This method insists on explaining correct usages informally. This method is effective in early stages when the pupils have not mastered enough of vocabulary.

**Limitations**

This method suffer from the following limitations: (a) All rules cannot be taught by this method; (b) Students do not get systematised knowledge of grammar; (c) It consumes much time and labour of students.

**(iii) The reference and correlation method**

It is also called incidental method. In this method, grammar is taught incidentally while teaching the text. While teaching the text or translating a passage or doing a composition, the teacher explains the grammatic rules, complex structures and their implications.

**Limitations**

This method suffers from the following limitations: (a) It is a not a complete method; (b) It may interfere with normal teaching

**(iv) Deductive method**

This method insists on rule first and examples later. The teacher gives the rule or definition of a grammatical item and then gives a number of examples from actions or pictures. Deductive means to proceed from law to observation. Traditional grammar is deductive in nature. The grammar of Wren and Martin and Nesfield is a good example. They give rules with examples and exceptions.

**Steps in Deductive Method**

Deductive method of teaching grammar includes two steps. They are: *(i)* application of the rule; and (ii) practice.

1. **Application of the rule:** The pupils learn the rules, study the examples given and apply the rules to do the exercises.
2. **Practice:** Teacher calls for more examples from the pupils. He provides adequate opportunity and exercises for practice.

**The Inductive Method**

This method is considered a good method because it is based on educational principles. This is an effective method in teaching of science. As grammar is a science of language, it is successfully used for teaching grammar. Inductive means proceeding from observation to law.

**Steps in Inductive Method**

The inductive method of teaching English includes the following four steps. They are: *(i)* presentation of examples and illustrations; *(ii)* analysis of examples; *(iii)* making generalisations; and *(iv)* forming rules.

**1. Presentation of examples and illustrations**

The teacher presents examples and illustrations in a systematic order, so that they may lead to generalisation. He can write the following sentences to teach how active voice is changed into passive voice on the blackboard.

I read a book →A book is read by me

They won the match →The match was won by them.

They will complete the work →The work will be completed by them.

2. **Analysis of examples**

He asks the pupils to point out the verb, subject and object in both types of sentences. He then asks them to point out the change in the verbs. In the end, he asks them to tell all the changes that they find in the second type of sentences.

3. **Making Generalisation:** When the students understand the changes mentioned above, they themselves come to certain conclusions

   *(i)* The object becomes the subject.

   *(ii)* The subject becomes the object and is preceded by the preposition by

The form of the verb changes. The past indefinite changes into the participle form.

4. **Forming rules**

After the students have pointed out the changes, the teacher tells them that these changes form the rules for changing active voice into passive voice.

The advocates of grammar say that knowledge of grammar enhances the confidence level as well as the competence level of the students in using the language in speech or writing. It fortifies the pupils against wrong usages and faulty constructions.

The critics of grammar, on the other hand, are very sceptic about the utility of grammar. They say, 'Away the rules; practise what is right again and again. They assert that many a great writer never studied grammar.

Both the views are extreme and can't be accepted. We should neither regard grammar as the most important part of language learning nor do away with it. Grammar should be taught as a means to an end and not as an end in itself. it should follow the language and not precede it. It should be picked up incidentally and almost unconsciously.

## TEACHING AIDS

Teaching aids are devices that present units of knowledge through auditory or visual stimulus or both with a view to enhance learning. Teaching aids make learning experience appear real, living and vital. They supplement the work of the teacher and help in the study of books.

### Need for Teaching Aids

Language deals with time both past and present, places in immediate vicinity as well as in distant corners of the world, people nearby as well as in different parts of the world. Mere chalking and talking will not help to make all these realistic and vivid before the pupils. Audio-visual aids will have to be used to make the teaching lively and interesting. To give a welcome relief from the normal routine, a variety of aids like pictures, maps, films, film strips, models, cartoons, charts, graphs etc should be drawn into the course.

### Objectives of Teaching Aids

The following are the primary objectives of teaching aids. Teaching aids are very essential

**1. To supplement the spoken word**

Teaching deals with words which go beyond the experience of pupils. Mere verbal descriptions do not help to drive home the facts to the pupils. The teacher must use teaching aids to supplement the spoken word.

**2. To make subject real and life like**

Aids make the subject appear real and life like. The use of teaching aids can add zest, interest and vitality to any teaching learning situation and make the subject understandable.

**3. To develop and improve attitudes and interests**

The presentation of teaching aids will help in portraying the matter in true and realistic form. This will lead to the development of proper concepts, improvement of attitudes and expression of appreciations and interests.

**4. To make learning permanent**

As teaching aids compel the pupils to be more attentive, they enable students to learn faster, remember longer, gain more accurate information.

5. **To supplement the text books**

Books lack the specificity, the warmth and poignancy of concrete experiences. Through teaching aids, the teacher can supply the context for sound and skillful generalising and help in better understanding of the text books.

**Types of Teaching Aids**

Teaching aids can be classified into two types as: *(i)* teacher made aids; and *(ii)* mechanical aids.

1. **Teacher made aids**: Teacher made aids are the aids made or prepared by the teacher to teach a particular concept.
2. **Mechanical aids**: Mechanical aids are machine based aids which require technical/mechanical knowledge on the part of the teachers to operate the aids.

**Audio Visual Aids**

Audio visual aids are the devices which increase the individual's experience beyond that acquired through reading by the dual effect of sight and sound. Its function is to arouse curiosity and to kindle interest about the extension, application and development of the topic in hand.

**Advantages of Audio Visual Aids**

What a visual presentation can do, any amount of verbal exposition cannot do. Audio visual aids penetrate more deeply into human character than any other medium. They transmit information from the point of origin to the point of reception with an immediate effect and excitement. They stimulate imagination and develop the pupils' power of observation. These aids may need explanation but they do not need translators. They speak a universal language of form, colour, position, motion etc. The following are the advantages of audio visual aids.

- They provide for adequate sensory experience required for understanding the concept.
- They provide substitutes for direct experiences to understand the new concepts, facts or symbols.
- They supplement the direct experiences by vicarious or representative learning.

- Audio visual aids have a motivating quality of their own as they possess vividness, clarity and dramatic appeal.
- These aids are extremely helpful to slow learners as they can easily understand and remember facts gained through pictures, movies, models, radio, TV etc.
- They facilitate memory storage, longer retention and smoother recall of information.
- They develop the power of imagination, observation, analysis and synthesis.
- They facilitate meaningful learning. Clear meaning provides deep learning. Audio visual aids provide meaning to each and everything used or displayed in the class.
- They break the monotony of the formal type of teaching.

**Correct Use of Audio Visual Aids**

The following are the guiding principles for the use of audio visual aids in the classroom.

- Audio visual aids should be used when required. They should not be used just for the sake of using.
- Teacher must use audio visual aids as means to an end.
- Audio visual aids must be simple and create genuine interest.
- It is always better to draw a map or sketch or a diagram before the students.
- Audio visual aids must be exhibited properly.
- Time, place and manner count a lot for effective use of audio visual aids.

## SUMMARY

Instructional objectives fall into three domains such as cognitive domain, affective domain and psychomotor domain. Cognitive domain consists of six classes or categories: Knowledge, comprehension, application, analysis synthesis and evaluation. Affective domain includes classes such as receiving, responding, valuing, conceptualisation, organisation and characterisation. The categories of psychomotor domain include imitation, manipulation, precision, coordination, naturalisation and habit formation.

Micro teaching is a teacher encounter in a real or simulated situation scaled down in time, in number of pupils and in scope of the content. It is a teacher training technique. Micro teaching skills include set induction or introduction, explanation, using the blackboard, stimulus variation, reinforcement, skill of questioning and demonstration. Link practice provides a bridge between micro teaching and macro teaching by increasing class size, teaching time, content and the skills.

Observation is the act of watching for a period of time to learn more about somebody or something. Perception, recording of what is observed, classification and analysis and generalisation are the stages of observation. There are various types of observation. There are specific measures to improve observation. Demonstration lesson is a lesson by the teacher educator or the guide teacher. English teachers need specific skills to play their role proficiently.

Macro teaching is the normal classroom teaching in real situation. Planning for instruction is a must. Pre teaching planning, planning during teaching and post teaching planning are the different stages of planning. Planning a lesson ensures systematic and orderly treatment of the subject matter and continuity in the teaching learning process. It enhances confidence and competence level of the teachers.

Prose is a meaningful unit with the best words in the best order. Various forms of prose are essay, novel, story, play, biography. travelogue etc. Prose is taught for acquisition of linguistic skills. Prose teaching includes procedures such as motivation or introduction, introduction of new grammatical structures, introduction of new vocabulary, model reading by the teacher, silent reading by the pupils, testing comprehension, word study, reading aloud by the pupils and giving assignment.

Poetry is musical or metrical form of language. Poems are taught for enjoyment, pleasure, appreciation, recitation and aesthetic sense development. Methods of teaching poetry include lecture method, question answer method, review method and meaning and understanding method. Teaching procedure includes introduction, presentation, model reading by the teacher, pronunciation drill, model reading II by teacher, explaining difficult words, model reading III by teacher, posing questions, chorus recitation and giving assignment.

Composition is a short text written as school exercise. Selection, gradation, oral practice, sequence and timely correction are the principles of teaching composition. There are two types of composition: oral composition and written composition. Written composition includes guided composition and free composition. Paragraph writing, paraphrasing, essay writing and descriptive writing are the various types of free composition.

Intensive reader is taught for acquisition of all the linguistic competencies. Usages of new structures, new words, pronunciation etc are much emphasised. Extensive reader is taught to create interest in reading for pleasure and to develop rapid silent reading skill. Criteria for selection of a reader are interesting subject matter, simple language, illustration, adequate activities, guidance to teachers and glossary.

Grammar is the theory of language and study of oragnisation of words into sentences. There are various types of grammar: formal grammar, functional grammar, structural grammar, transformational generative grammar and communicative grammar. Methods of teaching grammar include traditional method, informal method, reference correlation method, and inductive deductive method.

Teaching aids are devices that present units of knowledge through auditory or visual stimulus or both with a view to enhance learning. Teacher made aids and mechanical aids are the types of teaching aids. Audio visual aids are the devices which increase the individuals' experience beyond that acquired through reading by the dual effect of sight and sound. They develop the power of imagination, observation, analysis and synthesis.

# 5 Resources in Teaching English

## TEACHING AIDS

Teaching aids are devices that present units of knowledge through auditory, visual stimulus or both. There are two kinds of teaching aids. They are: *(i)* teacher made aids; and *(ii)* mechanical aids.

### Teacher Made Aids

Teacher made aids are the aids prepared by the teachers to ensure effective teaching learning process. Teaching aids supplement the work of the teachers. They provide for better teaching learning process. The important teacher made aids are discussed below:

**Reading cards:** Reading cards are used to teach children beginning to read. Matching cards are used. Children should match the picture with the word. There are two types of reading cards. They are non correcting cards and self correcting cards.

**Flash cards:** Flash cards help teachers to give practice to learners in recognition of words. Flash cards can be used to introduce new words. They can be used for teaching vocabulary and structure. Flash cards may have only picture with or without words. Or it may have phrase or sentence without picture. This may be used to facilitate silent reading and understanding.

**Charts:** Charts are collection of pictures on heavy paper or board. Charts can include diagrams, graphs, tables facts and figures. Charts are very useful to give oral practice. They enhance attention. They stimulate mental activity. Charts can be used for pattern practice. These types of charts are called pattern practice charts.

**Picture cards:** Printed picture cut from magazine or newspaper mounted on a piece of cardboard is called picture card. It enables the students to see and speak. It saves teacher time.

**Picture sets:** It refers to a sequence of pictures. It is used to tell stories. Teachers can show the pictures and ask the students to describe and narrate the story. Sequence of pictures in the form of film strip can be projected on the wall or screen.

**Wall pictures:** Wall pictures are large pictures. They provide practice in question and answer work. Map and phonetic charts are good examples. Phonetic charts are very useful to teach right pronunciation and to correct pronunciation.

**Flannel cut-outs:** Flannel cut outs are pictures mounted on a piece of cardboard with 1″ × 1″ sand paper affixed at the back.

**Models:** Models are three dimensional representations of real things. A model may be large or small or the same size as the object it represents. Plastic models of all types are available. There are models which can be assembled by students.

**Types of models:** There are two types of models i.e. working models and non working models.

### Teaching with Models

Teacher should know how to use models effectively in the classroom. To be successful in using models:

- Teacher should be familiar with the model.
- Teacher should practise his presentation with the model.
- If it is a working model, teacher should know how to operate.
- Teacher should encourage students to operate/handle the models.
- When not used, models should not be left in the classroom as it would distract the students.

### Uses of Models

1. Models can be used when realism is essential for learning.
2. Three dimensional representation (size, shape, colour) gives a realistic look.
3. In language teaching models are used for teaching new words.
4. Pictures should be visible to the whole class.

### Chalkboard

These boards may be yellow, black or while. Chalkboard is used for illustration. Teachers should possess illustrative skill. They should use chalkboard as frequently as possible. Teacher must be able to draw map, charts, diagram, outlines, graphs, tables etc to promote better teaching learning. Chalkboard is an effective visual aid.

### Effective Use of Chalkboard

1. Chalkboard should be clean without needless distractions.
2. Teacher should write in straight rows from left to right.
3. Large letters and drawings will attract attention of the students.
4. **Posture:** Teacher should not cover up the material on the board by standing infront of it.
5. **Brevity:** Teacher should be precise and write important points only.
6. **Talk to the class:** Teacher should talk to the students, not the board.
7. **Plan:** Teacher should plan ahead what to write on the board.
8. **Gather Tools:** Teacher should gather everything needed for writing before going to the class.
9. **Location:** Chalk board should not be too high or too low. It should be well higher.
10. **Saving Time:** Teacher should put complex matter on Board before the class meets. This saves teacher time.

### Mechanical Aids

Aids used with the help of machines are mechanical aids. The following are the important mechanical aids.

## Overhead Projector and Transparency

Overhead projectors project what the teacher has written on the transparent plastic film. Teacher need not write on the board. It saves time. Teacher will get more time for planning and preparation. It is useful for language teacher to provide pattern practice.

**Motion pictures:** Motion picture refers to moving pictures combined with second. It is a powerful visual aid. There are a number of motion pictures for teaching English. Motion pictures can be used to teach pronunciation, spelling, structures, conversation, pattern practice, recitation etc. It can be effectively used in language lab.

**Advantages:**

1. Motion pictures have more instructional value than any other aid
2. They train the ears and help in correct speech habits.
3. It looks real and provides direct experience to students.
4. Students learn better than from the textbook.
5. What a visual presentation can do, any amount of verbal explanation cannot do.

**Opaque Projector:** It is an improved projector. We can project any material on the screen. This needs darkroom. It may affect chalkboard use. Photographs, charts, pages of books can be projected.

**The Radio:** Radio is very useful for teaching and learning of English. Listening to radio lessons in English helps in developing correct pronunciation, intonation etc. Teacher can pose question to check the understanding of the students.

**Television:** Television is a multimedia aid. It is useful to learn pronunciation intonation etc. There are educational CDs and cassettes for learning English. Many educational programmes including programmes on teaching and learning of English are telecast now-a-days.

**Tape Recorder:** It is an audio aid. It produces sound. It is useful to develop listening skill and to provide pronunciation practice. They can listen to dialogues and speech. Audio cassettes and CDs are available for learning English.

**Lingua phone:** It is a long thin plate fixed at one end. It can be used for teaching pronunciation, stress and intonation. It can be made as a talking textbook. There are special records. Each record covers the works of four complete units.

## PROGRAMMED INSTRUCTION

According to Edgar Dale, "*Teaching is a broad, vague, ill defined term and instruction is a purposeful, orderly controlled sequencing of experiences to reach a specified goal. All instruction involves teaching but all teaching cannot be instruction.*" Programmed instruction involves controlled, carefully specified and skillfully arranged learning experiences. They are self instructional and self corrective.

According to Harold W Bernad, "*Programmed learning refers to the arrangement of instructional materials in progressive sequences.*"

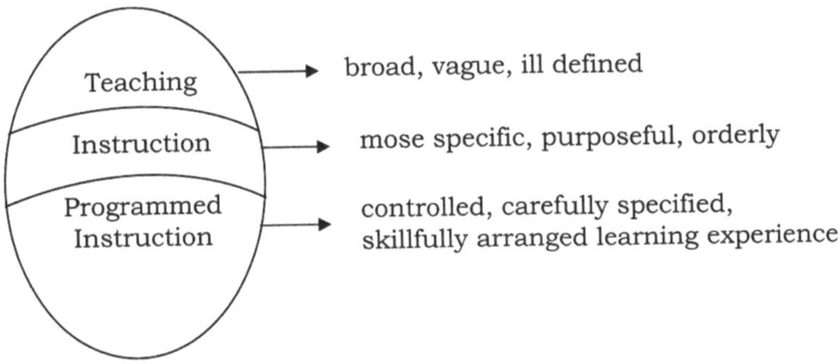


**What is programmed instruction?**

Programmed instruction is a technique of self instruction in which all of the instructional load is carried by teaching machines or programmed texts. Programmed instruction is a new path towards automation and individualised instruction.

**Characteristics of Programmed Instruction**

1. It is a method of individualised instruction
2. Subject matter is presented in a logical sequence.
3. It facilitates an active interaction between the learner and the programme.
4. Programmed learning provides immediate knowledge of result.

5. It includes organised nature of knowledge from easy to difficult.
6. The learner moves at his own pace.
7. There is constant evaluation in programmed instruction
8. It is a teaching method, not a test
9. It is not a teaching aid. It is not a panacea.

**Fundamental Principles**

The following are the fundamental principles of programme instruction:

1. **Small steps:** A programme is made up of a large number of small and easy steps. Students learn better in small steps.
2. **Active response:** Programmed learning is based on the principle of active response. Students learn better when they respond actively.
3. **Immediate knowledge of result:** As the student responds, his answer is confirmed immediately. Immediate confirmation serves as a kind of motivation or reinforcement.
4. **Self-pacing:** In programmed learning each student proceeds at his own pace. It is not time but mastery learning that is important.
5. **Constant evaluation:** There is constant evaluation in programmed learning. It helps students to learn and grasp the material given in each frame.

**Assumptions:** Students learn better.

1. When the subject matter is presented in small steps
2. Where there is active response
3. When there is immediate knowledge of result
4. When the content is presented in a logical sequence, and
5. Where is constant evaluation.

**Objectives**

The important objectives of programmed instruction are:

1. To help student to learn by doing
2. To provide the situation to learn at his own pace
3. To help student to learn without the presence of a teacher.

4. To present the content in a controlled manner and in logically related steps.
5. To study by himself and to assess his own performance by comparing it with the given answer.

**Types of Programmes**

There are three types of programming. They are:

*(i)* linear programme; *(ii)* branching programme; *(iii)* mathetics programme

**Linear Programme**

Skinner and his associates are the originators of linear programme. A linear programme is called a straight line programme. The learner starts from his initial behaviour to the terminal behaviour following a straight line. The student proceeds from one frame to the next until he completes the programme. The responses of the students are immediately reinforced in the succeeding frame.

**Branching Programme**

Branching programme was developed by Norman. A Crowder. It is called intrinsic programme. In this type, each frame is bigger. It contains two or three ideas of related sequence. Multiple choice type question is asked at the end. The student selects the response. If his answer is correct, he will proceed to the next frame in the main sequence. If wrong, he is taken to a remedial frame. His mistake is explained. After remedial work, he goes to the original frame and chooses the right answer. All the learners do not follow the same path. Error anticipation and error remediation are the main features of branching programme. Diagrammatically branching programme can be represented as follows.

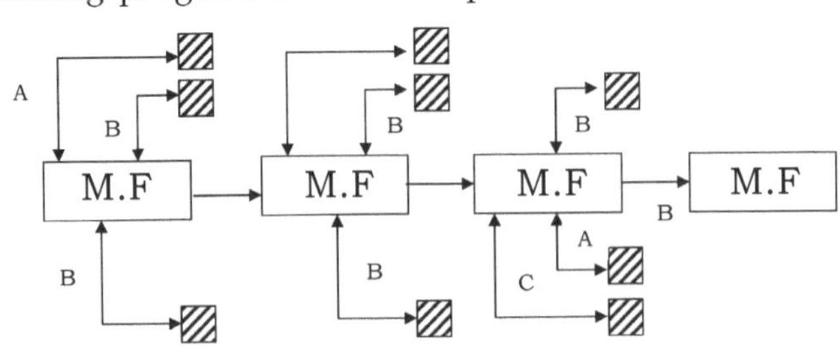

**Types of Branching Programme**

There are two types of branching programme. They are: *(i)* backward branching; *(ii)* forward branching.

**Backward Branching**

The learner goes from first frame to second frame if he makes correct response. If he makes an error, he is led to a remedial frame. He is remediated and then directed to the original frame. It is backward branching.

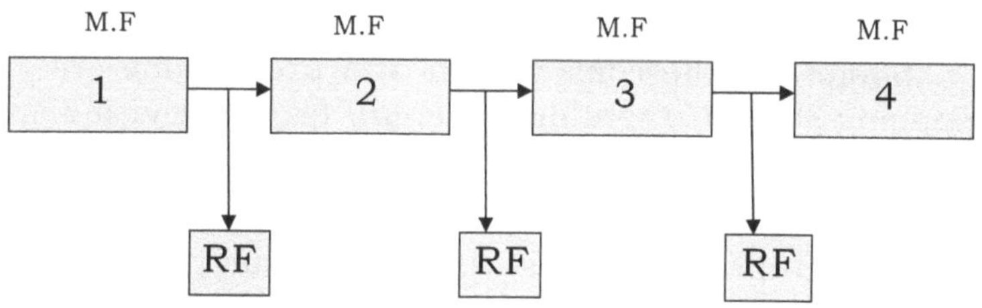


**Forward Branching**

In forward branching after remedial frame the learner proceeds to the next frame.

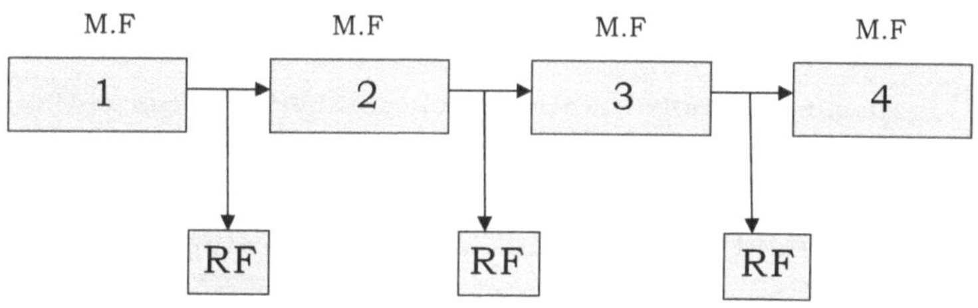


**Mathetics Programming**

Thomas F. Gilbert formulated the concept of mathetics. Mathetics is the systematic application of reinforcement theories to analysis and construction of knowledge or subject matter. The basic steps are: *(i)* data collection and task analysis; *(ii)* Prescription for mastery; *(iii)* characterisation and lesson plan; *(iv)* exercising writing; *(v)* editing.

**Stages of Programme Development**

Programme development includes three stages – They are: *(i)* preparation; *(ii)* constructing or writing the programme/construction stage; *(iii)* Evaluation stage.

**(i) Preparation Stage**

Preparation stage includes the following seven steps:

1. Selection of a topic (unit) to be programmed
2. Writing assumptions about learners
3. Defining objectives in behavioural terms
4. Defining pre-requisite skills in behavioural terms
5. Writing a criterion test
6. Developing the content outline.

**(ii) Construction or writing stage**

Stages for the construction of a programme are: *(i)* Planning stage; *(ii)* writing stage; *(iii)* testing, revising and editing stage.

**(iii) Evaluation stage**

1. The programmer must list basic assumptions about learners in objective and concrete terms.
2. He should describe the age, gender, skills, interests and ambitions of the learners.
3. He may judge the ability of the learners from the scores obtained in intelligence test, aptitude test, achievement test etc.
4. He should know the socio-economic status of his learners.
5. He should know the educational level of the parents of the learners.
6. He should be quite frank in writing assumptions about learners.
7. He should not be concerned about its length or its literary style.

## LANGUAGE LAB

A language laboratory is a separate room where the students can practise speaking and listening with the aid of computers, tape recorders, ear phones, microphones and other sound equipments. Language lab is specially designed for teaching of languages. It contains play back and recording equipment for the students to practise the language. Lab provides good models of speech.

**How to use language lab?**

1. Teacher should select and prepare the material with care
2. Teacher should explain the operations
3. Materials should be clear, graded and purposeful
4. Teacher should check the performance of students.
5. There should be provision for self correction
6. Good models for pronunciation, stress and intonation should be provided.
7. More emphasis must be laid on listening skills.

**Limitations**

1. It is more difficult and expensive to produce good materials
2. The prepared materials soon become outdated
3. Teacher cannot spend more time on preparation, administration and evaluation.

## COMPUTER ASSISTED INSTRUCTION (CAI)

Any instruction imparted or presented through computer is called computer assisted instruction. It refers to the use of computer as an integral part in the instructional system.

**Basic Assumptions of CAI**

1. More students can learn simultaneously. There is use of structured curriculum.
2. An individual can learn at his own pace.
3. There is immediate and personalised feedback.
4. All subjects can be covered. It provides for individualised instruction.

**Various Modes of CAI**

There are different modes of CAI. The most important of them are: *(i)* tutorial CAI; *(ii)* Drill and practice CAI; *(iii)* Generative CAI; *(iv)* Dialogue enquiry CAI; *(v)* Simulation CAI

1. **Tutorial CAI:** Information is presented in small units followed by questions. If the student gives correct answer, the computer gives further information. If the student gives wrong answer, the computer gives feedback/supplementary information. After the student

gives the right answer, the computer advances on the main programme and gives further information and puts question.

2. **Drill and practice CAI:** In this mode, the programme leads the learner through a series of examples to develop dexterity and fluency in using the skill. All correct responses are reinforced. After the student achieves mastery, the computer will proceed further.
3. **Generative CAI:** In this mode computer is programmed to generate questions within a basic frame work about the topic. Questions are generated depending on the previous answer of the student.
4. **Dialogue/Enquiry CAI:** This mode permits students to conduct a limited dialogue with the computer. The student puts questions and the computer answers and vice versa.
5. **Simulation CAI:** Simulation involves creating a real life-like situation for the purpose experimentation and observation. Science experiments can be simulated. Experiments too dangerous to perform can be simulated. Experiments requiring long period can be simulated.

**Other modes:**

Other modes are gaming mode, problem solving mode, author mode and logo.

**Advantages of CAI**

CAI refers to using computer in teaching learning process. It does not mean teaching people to use computer. The advantages of CAI are:

1. It provides for individualisation of instruction.
2. It caters to individual differences. Students can learn at their own rate or pace.
3. It makes use of structured curriculum. There is logical sequence in presentation of information
4. The immediate personalised feedback facilitates better learning. It provides reinforcement at right time
5. It has a movating quality of its own.

**Limitations of CAI**

Though highly valued, CAI is not without limitations.

1. It fails to appreciate the emotions of the students
2. CAI programmes do not in themselves solve pshychological or educational problems. Some students become fatigued.
3. CAI fails to develop essential language competency where ability to generate or construct meaningful sentences is required.
4. It cannot appreciate the students' artistic endeavour
5. The operational constraints retard the interaction of students with computer.

## MULTIMEDIA

Multimedia, or mixed – media, systems offer presentations that integrate effects existing in a variety of formats, including text, graphics, animation, audio, and video. Such presentations first became commercially available in very primitive form in the early 1980s, as a result of advances that have been made in digital compression technology particularly the difficult area of image compression. Multimedia online services are obtainable through telephone/computer or television links. Multimedia hardware and software exist for personal computers, networks, the internet, interactive kiosks and multimedia presentations are available on CD-ROMs and various other mediums. The use of multimedia in our society has it is benefits and its drawbacks, most defiantly. Some of the more computer-related uses of multimedia are electronic publishing, the internet, and computers in education.

Multimedia presentation refers to transmitting of information to the pupils through more than one medium in a single communication either sequentially or simultaneously. Multimedia instructional strategy refers to the instructional strategy which incorporates minimum two or more than two media in its instructional process so as to enable the pupils to achieve the predetermined educational objectives. Multimedia presentation can penetrate more deeply into human character with an immediate effect and excitement than any other single medium. The dual effect of audio and video strengthens and enriches the understanding and expedites the mastery of the concept.

## INTERNET

In a very short time, the internet has become a major vehicle of worldwide communication and an unrivaled source of information. One of the internet's fascinations is that its resources are limited only by the number of computers participating in the World Wide Web and the imaginations of the users.

The Internet is an international web of interconnected government, education, and business computer networks - in essence, a network of networks. From a thousand or so networks in the mid-1980s, the Internet had grown to about 30,000 connected networks in mid-1994. By mid-1995 the number of networks had doubled to more than 60,000, making the Internet available to an estimated 40 million people worldwide.

The Internet is also a repository of information for business. Thousands of discussion groups with specialised interests in topics ranging from aeronautics to molecular biology share data across the internet. The US government posts more and more information, such as commerce department data and new patent filings, on the internet. Additionally, many universities are converting large libraries to electronic form for distribution on the internet. One of the most ambitious examples is Cornell University's ongoing project to convert 100,000 books, printed over the past century, on the development of American infrastructure books on bridges, roads, and other public works.

### Merits

- The greatest merit of Internet is that it opens a world of information at the press of a key. It helps to gather information from storage areas of the servers called websites. Today we can get any information on any topic in a matter of seconds.
- We can visit libraries situated thousands of miles away, enjoy world famous sights which we have only imagined,

talk to people, listen to lectures, read the day's newspapers, transact business, place orders, etc. just sitting in our room. Internet can provide the latest information on education, sports, entertainment, science, medicine, general knowledge etc. in seconds.

- Internet has improved our communication system. It has provided an exciting and easy mode of communication known as E-Mail (Electronic Mailing system). Today we can send letters and mails to anyone living in any part of the world just by clicking a few buttons on our computer and that too at an extremely cheap rate.
- Not only letters can be sent but, we can also chat with our near and dear ones, see them before our eyes just sitting in our room. Internet has made communication, highly fast, cheap, safe, and least cumbersome.
- It's educative and entertainment value is also very great. Internet has also widened business opportunities. You can advertise your goods and products in the internet as well as seek jobs, place orders, meet with business magnates, attend international business conferences, deal with stock market, buy and exchange currencies, transact bank business, etc., and thus it is known as electronic commerce or E-Commerce.

**A word of caution**

- Although, Internet immensely helps man in his day-to-day transactions, it is a tool that is often misused. Today thousands of youth are getting 'hooked' to Internet watching things which are not meant for them.
- Electronic pornography is ruining our youth. Electronic crimes, illegal piracy into private lives and military software, creating new type of computer virus etc, have become quite common now-a-days.
- Internet hankers (those who try to block the working of other internets) are on the rise, creating havoc in the world of business and communication. Too much dependence of man on this man-made machine is also ruining man's innate qualities.

Internet is a great tool which man has invented. Its potential is still not fully tapped. More and more uses of Internet are being discovered as days go by. It has made our life easy, comfortable, pleasurable and luxurious. Internet has ushered in the cyber age. However, it is high time that its wrong use and negative impact be minimised. If not put an end to, it will strangle our young generation and lead them to moral abyss.

## POWER POINT PRESENTATION

It refers to the presentation of graphics, text, drawings, charts, graphs, slides etc through microsoft powerpoint. We can give transition effects and animation affects. It can reach an audience of large size. It includes four steps such as planning, preparing, practising and presenting.

## IDENTIFYING WEBSITES

Internet is a global library. It provides information on countless topics. There are procedures to locate the required websites. The best resource to identify websites is directories. Directories are collection of resources organised into categories. Important directories are:

1. The internet public library – http://www.ipl.org
2. Look Smart – http://www.looksmart.com
3. The Open Directory – http://dmoz.org
4. Web Brain – http://www.webbrain.com
5. Yahooligans – http://www.yahooligans.com

## SEARCH ENGINES

An internet search engine explores information across the internet and collects copies of web pages from various hot servers. Some important search engines are:

| | |
|---|---|
| Google | www.google.com |
| Search Bug | www.searchbug.com |
| Alta Vista | www.altavista.com |
| Lycos | www.lycos.com |
| Northern Light | www.northenlight.com |
| All the web | www.altheweb.com |
| Hot Bot | www.hotbot.com |
| Metacrawler | www.goznet.com |

## SUMMARY

Teaching aids are devices that present units of knowledge through auditory, visual stimulus or both. Teacher made aids and mechanical aides are the two kinds of teaching aids. Teaching aids supplement the work of the teachers. They provide for better teaching learning process.

Teacher made aids are the aids prepared by the teachers to ensure effective teaching learning process. The important teacher made aids are reading cards, flash cards, charts, picture cards, picture sets, wall pictures, flannel cut-outs, chalkboard and both working and non-working models.

Mechanical aids are the aids used with the help of machines. The important mechanical aids include overhead projector and transparency, opaque projector, radio, television, tape recorder and lingua phone. To make use of mechanical teaching aids teachers should know how to operate.

Programmed instruction is a technique of self instruction in which all of the instructional load is carried by teaching machines or programmed texts. Characteristics of programmed instruction are individualisation, logical sequence, active interaction between the learner and the programme, immediate knowledge of result, constant evaluation and one's own pace of learning.

Fundamental principles of programmed instruction include small steps, active response, immediate knowledge of result, self pacing and constant evaluation. There are three types of programming: linear programme, branching programme and mathetics programme. Forward branching and backward branching are the two types of branching programme.

Programme development includes three stages. They are preparation stage, construction stage and evaluation stage. Construction stage includes three sub-stages namely planning stage, writing stage and testing, revising and editing stage. Preparation stage includes seven steps.

A language laboratory is a separate room where the students can practise speaking and listening with the help of computers, tape recorders, ear phones, microphones and other sound equipments. Effective use of language lab will facilitate adequate development of communicative skills.

Any instruction imparted or presented through computer is called computer assisted instruction. It refers to the use of computer as an integral part in the instructional system. There are different modes of CAI. The most important modes are tutorial CAI, drill and practice CAI, generative CAI, dialogue enquiry CAI, simulation CAI etc.

Multimedia, or mixed media systems offer presentations that integrate effects existing in a variety of formats, including text, graphics, animation, audio and video. The dual effect of audio and video strengthens and enriches the understanding and expedites the mastery of the concept.

Internet is an international web of interconnected government, education and business computer networks, in essence, a network of networks. It is a major vehicle of worldwide communication and an unrivalled source of information. More and more uses of internet are being discovered as days go by.

The best resource to identify websites is directories. Directories are collection of resources organised into categories. There are various directories for this purpose. An internet search engine explores information across the internet and collects copies of web pages from various hot servers.

# 6

# Approaches and Methods of Teaching English

## SYLLABI IN ENGLISH LANGUAGE TEACHING

**Syllabus:** syllabus is an outline and summary of topics to be covered in a course. It is often either set by an exam board, or prepared by the professor who teaches the course. It is usually given to each student during the first class session.

### Function of a Syllabus

"A language teaching syllabus involves the combination of subject matter (what to teach) and linguistic matter (how to teach) It actually performs as a guide for both teacher and learner by providing some goals to be accomplished. Syllabus, in fact, deals with linguistic theory and theories of language learning and how they are utilised in the classroom (Mohseni, 2008)

### Types of English Syllabi

There are various types of English syllabi. They are: *(i)* cultural syllabus; *(ii)* situational syllabus; *(iii)* structural or formal syllabus; *(iv)* task based syllabus; *(v)* Learner – led syllabus; *(vi)* content based syllabus; and *(vii)* lexical syllabus.

1. **Cultural syllabus:** The syllabus that gives much importance to various aspects of culture is called cultural syllabus.

The aim of this syllabus is to teach the following about culture:

- ❖ to develop an adequate knowledge about the target culture.

- to create awareness of its characteristics and of the differences between the target culture and other cultures.
- This syllabus lays emphasis on understanding of socio cultural implications of language and language use (Mohseni, 2008).

2. **Situational syllabus:** The syllabus that gives much importance to use of situations in teaching and learning of a language is called situational syllabus:
   - This syllabus stresses the use of situations to guide language teaching because language is related to situational contexts in which it occurs (Mohseni, 2008)
   - The main principle of situational language teaching syllabus is to teach the language that occurs in the situations
   - Language skills are acquired for the purpose of situational use or use in context.
   - This syllabus merges pronunciation, vocabulary, grammar with listening to language with a purpose: writing and speaking.
   - The purpose of the syllabus is for the ELL to develop language skills.
3. **Structural or formal syllabus**
   - This is a multidimensional traditional syllabus that focuses on language forms.
   - This syllabus tries to develop an insight into structural complexity, difficulty, regularity, utility and frequency.
   - The learner is expected to master each structural step and add it to his/her grammar collection.
   - This is done through highly controlled, highly structured and sequenced pattern practice.
4. **Task based syllabus**

It is called process syllabus. Tasks and activities are used to promote language learning.

- This syllabus stresses the application and practice of language

- The most important point is that the tasks must be relevant to the real world language needs of the learner. It should be a meaningful task so as to enhance learning.
- This syllabus is designed in an ongoing way according to students' wants
- This syllabus provides opportunities for alternative procedures and activities for the classroom group.

5. **Learner – led syllabus**
   - The instructor uses a prearranged syllabus, but the learners create and modify the syllabus to develop language skills.
   - This syllabus stresses the use of theme within a unit, chosen by the learner to emphasise language form and then shift to language interaction.
   - This syllabus is appropriate and applicable to learners who lack exposure to the target language beyond the classroom.
   - This syllabus tries to develop overall competence
6. **Content based syllabus**
   - In this syllabus subject matter is of primary importance, but language learning occurs along with content.
   - Some linguistic adjustments may need to be made to make content understandable.
   - This syllabus lays emphasis on purpose of communication and meaning of language.
   - Needs analysis is needed in order to create the syllabus.
7. **Lexical Syllabus**
   - This syllabus makes a specific focus on vocabulary, specific words, and phrases that frequently appear in books and conversations.
   - This syllabus stresses learning from examining corpus of language or sentences.
   - By exposing learners to carefully selected language and by arming them with analysing that language for themselves, the syllabus helps the learners to achieve their goals successfully.

**What type of syllabus to use?**

- It depends on how we teach. No single type of syllabus is appropriate for all teaching setting. We should use multiple types.
- The question is not which type to choose but which types and how to connect them with each other or one another.
- When choosing a syllabus design, we should take into account all the potential factors that may affect the teachability of a specific syllabus.

## METHODS AND APPROACHES

Approach is a way of dealing with somebody or something: Method is a particular way of doing things, Strategy is an intended plan to achieve something, Technique is a tactic employed to achieve something, Design is a sketch for a work to be executed.

### Characteristics of Good Method/Approach

A good method or approach should have the following characteristics.

It should achieve maximum objectives.

It should suit different age groups.

It should be capable of teaching language and literature.

It should follow the principles of teaching.

It should be suitable for small and large size classes.

## METHODS OF TEACHING ENGLISH

There are various methods of teaching English. They are grammar translation method, bilingual method, direct method and Dr. West's new method.

### Grammar Translation Method

It is called classical method. It was introduced by the British –It has no psychological basis but it has the following philosophical basis (i.e) It is easy to learn through mother tongue. Grammar is soul of a language.

### Procedure

Teacher translates. He gives mother tongue equivalent. It is the oldest method. Textbook occupies an important place. The textbook has all the reading materials, specific graded vocabulary, rules of grammar and some new words in every lesson.

**Characteristics of Grammar Translation Method**

Word is unit of teaching. Mother tongue dominates the teaching learning process. More emphasis is laid on grammar rules.

**Merits of the Translation Method**

It is economical, it saves time and it enhances vocabulary of the pupils. It promotes clear understanding. Old and new ideas are connected in this method. It proceeds from known to unknown. It facilitates correct language acquisition. Aids are not much essential. It develops translation skill. It helps in making comprehension. It can be used in all situations. It is suitable for language classes.

**Demerits of the Translation Method**

Speaking, reading, writing skills are neglected. It fails to teach pronunciation, intonation. Some words and idioms and phrases cannot be translated. It encourages literal translation which is not advisable. It prevents independent thinking. If affects students interest. It is against the principle *from whole to part*. It neglects silent reading and rapid reading. It teaches language by rules. It is dull and an uninteresting method.

**Bilingual Method**

Bilingual Method uses both English and mother tongue. It lays much emphasis on pattern practice based on similarities and differences between mother tongue and English. Mother tongue is used for making the meanings of word clear. Then pattern practice is provided to students.

**Principles of Bilingual Method**

Meanings can be made clear with the help of the mother tongue. Use of mother tongue saves time of the teacher. Time saved can be used for practice.

**Advantage**

English can be taught to the entire satisfaction of the learners. It develops all skills –It saves a lot of time. It develops fluency. It ensures accuracy. No special facilities or equipments are needed to make the teaching learning process more effective. It is a pleasant way for the teacher to help. It banks upon mother tongue. It makes use of the language habits acquired by the learners while learning their mother tongue.

### Disadvantages

This method confuses and diverts the attention of students. This method requires the teacher to have skill in both English and mother tongue. Otherwise, teaching learning process cannot be effective. Use of mother tongue affects fluency. It leads to literal translation. Defective habits of learning may be formed. Teaching may degenerate into translation.

### Direct Method

This method originated in France in 1901. It is called reformed method. To teach English direct association between experience and expression must be established. It is a method of teaching language through conversation, discussion and reading. There is no use of mother tongue and formal grammar. Words are taught by using object, pictures or actions. Direct bond between word and meaning is established. This method enables students to think and speak in English.

### Essential Features of Direct Method

It follows the principles of proceeding from concrete to abstract.

- Translation is avoided in any form
- Meanings of words are taught by objects, models and actions.
- Oral work precedes reading and writing
- Grammar is taught indirectly
- Unit of speech is a sentence, not a word
- The words are directly associated with the things they stand for
- Object, pictures, models, actions are used for teaching words
- Adequate pattern practice is provided in classroom situation

### Advantages of Direct Method

Direct method has the following advantages:

- This method facilitates understanding without use of mother tongue.

- It is a natural method. Language is taught through demonstration and conversation. Listening leads to speaking.
- It promotes fluency of speech. There is more stress on oral work. There is no effect of mother tongue. It develops confidence. Students think in English and use English with correct pronunciation.
- This method facilitates reading and writing. It makes study of English easy and pleasant.
- It makes more use of AV aids.
- In this method, sentence is unit of teaching, not word.
- It promotes critical study of English literature.
- It helps to cover more portion in less time
- This method is psychologically sound. It proceeds from particular to general and from concrete to abstract.

**Disadvantages**

The following are the disadvantages of the direct method:

- There is lack of atmosphere. The atmosphere created does not last long.
- It is incomplete method. It promotes oral aspects. It neglects reading and writing. Hence it is an incomplete method.
- There is lack of suitable teachers. Skilled teachers are rare. Most of the teachers have poor command and expression. They are marked for faulty pronunciation.
- It is a difficult and expensive method. AV aids cost much.
- It does not suit all students and all schools.
- It is laborious method. It needs much time for preparation,
- There is no systematic teaching of grammar in this method.

**Reasons for its Unpopularity**

Direct method became unpopular due to following reasons:

- There is shortage of skilled teachers

- There is lack of proper facilities. AV aids are not adequate. The classrooms are overcrowded. Teaching materials are not sufficient.
- Teachers themselves were trained by translation method. So they are not able to apply this method successfully.

**Conclusion**

This method is suitable for early stages. It is not suitable for higher stages. It is of course, better than translation method. It can be used with other methods for better results.

**Dr. West's New Method**

W.P. West, principal of training college, Dacca, was the director of education in prepartition Bengal. West proposed this method. In this method limitations of direct method were removed.

**Need for English Education**

English education promotes internationalism and universal brotherhood

- English is still the *lingua franca* in India among states
- No Indian language is rich in the field of science
- There is much emphasis on development of reading and vocabulary.

**Salient Features**

Salient features of Dr. West's is new method include the following:

- There is much on emphasis on developing reading ability.
- Silent reading is very essential. It leads to self learning by reading.
- Reading leads to learning to speak and write.
- Grammar is not a code of rules.

**Procedure**

- West designed reading books.
- Vocabulary is strictly controlled.
- Vocabulary is selected according to mental development.
- Frequently used words are selected.
- New word is introduced carefully and is used again and again in different contexts.
- Forms words and content words are adequately covered.

**Advantages**

The advantages of Dr. West's new method are:

- This method promotes comprehension, correct pronunciation, etc.
- It lays much emphasis on silent reading.
- Both readings promote self learning.
- It makes writing easy.
- There is not much stress on phonetics.
- There is no overload of grammatical rules.
- Limited use of mother tongue is very useful.
- It develops a taste for English literature.
- It is an economical method in terms of time and money.

**Disadvantages**

- This method ignores the other skills. For ex, listening, speaking and writing.
- It is not psychologically sound.
- Reading becomes dull and monotonous.
- West gives more importance to reading than to speaking. His opinion is wrong.
- This method is not enough for short stories and long stories.
- Readers are bulky.
- This method overlooks sub –couscious efforts.
- Grammar, composition, idioms are neglected in this method.

## APPROACHES

Approach is a way of dealing with things. There are various approaches to teach English. The important approaches are: *(i)* structural approach; *(ii)* situational approach; *(iii)* oral approach; *(iv)* structural, oral, situational approach; *(v)* communicative approach; and *(vi)* eclectic approach.

**Structural Approach**

The approach based on teaching and learning of structures is called structural approach. British Council Institute of Education, University of London, proposed this approach, It is based on the study of structures. Mastery of structure is essential for learning any language. Patterns of words are called structures. Structures are tools of a language

**Four Types of Structures**

There are four types of structures. They are:

- Sentence pattern
- Phrase pattern
- Idioms and
- Formulas

Structural approach refers to teaching and learning of English on the basis of structures.

Language can be learnt through study of words and structures

**Basic Principles**

This approach stresses the importance of speech. Speech is more important. It develops other skills. Mastery of structures is more important. It leads to speaking, reading, writing. Formation of habits is very much emphasised. Language learning is a process of habits formation. Drill and practice should be provided till the concepts/structures are fixed up in the mind.

- This approach gives much importance to activities. Learning by doing is emphasised.
- Meaningful situation is essential for creating interest
- Teaching one item at a time is the golden rule. New structure is taught by using known vocabulary

**Characteristics of Structural Approach**

The following are the characteristics of structural approach:

- This approach gives importance to speech.
- This lays emphasis on forming language habits.
- Creating meaningful situations is very important.
- Emphasis is laid on student activity.
- Proper selection and gradation of structures should be followed.

### Aims of Structural Approach

The important aims of structural approach are:

- To teach English through 275 graded structures by means of drill and practice.
- To enable students to learn 3000 words.
- The correlate teaching of grammar and composition.
- To develop LSRW skills in the same order.
- To lay proper emphasis on aural –oral approach.

### Procedure

Structural approach includes the following procedure:

- We should present an item in appropriate situation.
- Then we should provide oral drill to students.
- Then the item should be used in new situation.
- Repetition and practice should be provided adequately.
- Over all drill is given to the students.

### Merits of Structural Approach

Merits of structural approach are:

- This approach lays emphasis on speech. Students practise structure by means of drill.
- It is suitable for all stages of education.
- There is creation of meaningful situation and appropriate environment.
- students cultivate habit of speaking.
- It can be used to teach prose, poetry, etc.
- Drill and practices fix the concept in mind.
- It provides ample opportunity for students to express their ideas feelings etc.
- It is based on scientific principles.
- This approach makes both teacher and students active.

### Demerits

The following are the demerits of the structural approach:

- This approach is suitable for lower classes only.
- Only well selected structures alone can be taught.
- It is not possible to teach prescribed textbook.
- It places too much emphasis on mechanical drilling.

- It cannot be used in over –crowed classes.
- Those who were trained in grammar translation method experience difficulty in using this method.
- More teaching aids are needed.
- It is difficult to complete the syllabus.
- This approach neglects reading skill, vocabulary expansion and exploitation of students knowledge of mother tongue.

**Principles of selection of structures:** The following principles should govern the selection of structure. Simplicity, utility, teach ability, productivity, difficulty level are the vital factors in selection of structures. The structures must be simple to teach and to learn. The utility of the structures will decide the priority of learning. The structure must be easily teachable.

The students must be able to use the structure on their own. It should be within the difficulty level of the students.

### Situational Approach

The approach that highlights the importance of situations in teaching and learning of English is called situational approach.

### Characteristics

The following are the characteristics of situational approach:

- Teacher individually introduces new words.
- He should create situation to make the meaning clear.
- Materials are used to create a situation.
- Constant repetition is stressed.
- Many examples in short duration are given.
- Teacher poses many questions based on situation.
- Revision is done again and again.
- Teacher can use objects available in the classroom.
- Classroom situation should be used effectively.
- Imperatives are to be used properly.
- Teacher should ask many questions.
- Mother tongue can be used only in the beginning.

**Merits of Situational Approach**

- It is based on the principle of interest.
- Action chain gears up activities.
- It follows the principle of variety and simplicity.
- It lays stress on learning by playing.
- It makes use of teaching aids.

**Demerits**

Demerits of the situational approach are as follows:

- It is effective only in teaching well selected words and structures.
- It is suitable for lower classes only.
- Drill and practice becomes monotonous.
- It is not effective in teaching prose, poetry and translation.
- It is not possible to use this approach without proper training.

**Oral Approach**

The approach that gives much importance to oral works in teaching learning process is called oral approach.

1. It is natural process of learning.
2. It begins with speech.
3. Hence it is psychologically sound.

**Main Considerations**

1. Speech leads to other habits.
2. Internalisation of grammar.
3. Child learns grammar unconsiously.

**Advantages**

1. It ensures economy of time and effort.
2. It is convenient to introduce from the beginning.
3. There is instant correction.
4. Correction is easy and effective.
5. It provides for development of two basic skills i.e. listening, speaking.
6. Automatic response gears up learning.
7. Motivating the slow learners is possible.
8. Easier evaluation provides for assessing strength and weakness.

**Disadvantages**

1. Correct pronunciation is a problem.
2. Sound does not reflect spelling.
3. There is lack of competent teachers.
4. Learners feel shy to participate.

**Structural, Oral, Situational Approach**

It is an approach evolved through the combination of structural approach, oral approach and situational approach.

**Basic Assumptions**

1. learning language is learning syntax, not words.
2. Vocabulary is presented through graded vocabulary list.
3. Skills are presented in LSRW order.
4. Sentence patterns exist. They form the basis for language course.

In 1950 it was followed is Tamil Nadu. Now there is a shift to communicative approach.

**Classroom Procedure**

It involves three phases. They are presentation phase, practice phase and production phase. In the presentation phase, new vocabulary and grammatical items are introduced. In the practice phase, there is controlled practice. Production stage marks the performance and competence of the students.

**Merits**

It helps to develop skill in using structures. Using language in appropriate situation makes learning easier and meaningful. Concrete items are taught through demonstration Abstract ideas are taught through association

**Drawbacks**

Situations are not real situations.

It is difficult to make abstract ideas understandable.

This is suitable at elementary level only, not for higher classes.

It is not effective in teaching prose, poetry and composition.

**Communicative Approach**

The approach that stresses the importance of communication in teaching and learning on English is called communicative approach.

- Language is a tool of communication.
- English language is a powerful means of communication.
- One can learn language by using it.
- It is a learner centred approach.
- It develops communicative skills as well as social skill.
- Accuracy and appropriateness are equally important in communicative approach.
- Communicative approach develops both accuracy and fluency.
- It is function based and task centred approach.
- Learner is given task he should perform the tasks.
- Teacher is a co-participant.

Principles

The principles governing the communicative approach are:

- Both context and meaning are important.
- Language learning means ability to communicate. Careful and judicious use of mother tongue is allowed.
- Reading and writing can be started simultaneously.
- Fluency and error free language are essential.
- Students should perform the task assigned.
- Pair work and group work are encouraged.

**Merits**

The following are the merits of the communicative approach:

- By interacting in pairs and in groups students learn better.
- Learning becomes a self generating exercise.
- Students get more language practice.
- They acquire fluency, accuracy and appreciate use of language.
- It leads to co-operative learning.

- This approach is situational, meaningful; and self awarding.

**Demerits**

Demerits of the communicative approach include:

- Overcrowded classroom makes group work difficult.
- Average teacher cannot use this approach successfully.
- Structure based syllabus is neglected as much importance is given to conversational session.

**Eclectic Approach**

The collection of all good points of different methods and then using them for teaching English is called eclectic approach.

## PROJECT METHOD

Projects are special tasks assigned to students. Projects offer students challenging activities.

**Steps**

**Selection**: selection of project is very important. Selection of project should be in tune with age and experience level of the students.

**Planning:** Planning is very essential to complete the work. Good planning is half done.

**Executing:** Project should be carried out with all care. Teacher simply guides.

**Evaluating:** After completing the project, it should be evaluated. We should see whether the outcomes serve our purpose.

**Merits**

Merits of the project method are:

- The child performs and evaluates his own work.
- The learners should assess the quality of their work.
- All the connected mental and physical activities lead them to learn better.
- It develops in students scientific attitude.

**Requirements**

The requirements of a project include:

- Students should keep – diary of their work.
- They should write the name of the project.
- Date and time, should be mentioned. Evaluation report should be written.

**Action Research**

- Action research is an action programme to find solution for a problem. It is a research undertaken by educational practitioners of local school /community.

**Need for Action Research**

Teachers, students and schools are benefited.

- It is required to cope with the inevitable changes.
- It is useful to find viable solution to problem encountered.
- Teachers should try to find new practical, economical methods suitable for local schools.
- The problems of speech, reading, oral and written expressions, discipline etc can be probed into.

**Challenges**

Action research is not without challenges. The challenges include:

- Teachers do not get proper guidance.
- Government does not provide fund.
- Teachers are overloaded with school works.

**Steps in Action Research**

Steps in action research include:

- Locating a problem
- Analysing the cause of the problem.
- Evolving a strategy to overcome the problem.
- Applying the strategy to provide remedy.
- Analysing the 'data'/outcome.
- Arriving at conclusion and generalisation.

## ACTIVITY BASED LEARNING

- It is a new approach in teaching and learning of English.
- English is taught through well designed and well developed cards.

- ❖ It simplifies the process of teaching and learning.
- ❖ It makes learning more logical and natural.
- ❖ Learning involves listening, speaking, reading, writing.
- ❖ It is like supporting a huge structure with four pillars.

**Procedure**

- ❖ Separate logos are arranged for each learning activity.
- ❖ Names of vehicles are logos for English.
- ❖ Same logos are given for same kind of activities.
- ❖ Logos are distributed in milestones. Each milestone has various stages.

**Activities included**

The following activities are included under each skill:

**Listening:** Rhymes, alphabets, words relating to home, school, greetings, responses conversation, commands, instructions, etc.

**Speaking:** Asking questions and answering, making polite requests, saying "Thank You "sorry "asking for permission, expressing needs etc.

**Reading**

Recognising lower and upper class letters.

Reading words with pictures

Reading words without pictures

**Writing**

Drawing and painting, Drawing lines and curves leading to writing, Letter writing, Writing words

## ACTIVE LEARNING METHODOLOGY

It is based on the principle of learning by doing. It stresses active involvement of students in learning process. The strategy promotes activities. The strategy that involves students in doing things and thinking about what they are doing is called active learning. Students are not simply listening but they do some activities including discovering, processing and applying information.

**Basic Assumption of ALM**

Learning is by nature our active endeavour. Different people learn in different ways.

**Five basic skills emphasized in ALM:** *(i)* Reading; *(ii)* Drawing a mind map; *(iii)* Summarising; *(iv)* Discussion; and *(v)* Writing.

**Procedure or steps:** *(i)* Browsing; *(ii)* reading; *(iii)* consolidation; and reinforcement; *(iv)* constructing knowledge; *(v)* mindmapping; *(vi)* Discussion; *(vii)* assessment; *(viii)* Remedial instruction; *(ix)* summarising.

**Advantages of ALM**

The advantages of ALM are:

- ALM ensures active engagement on child's part.
- It provides a template for learning and learning to learn.
- Child is not subjected to endless passivity.
- ALM is applicable in large classroom and schools with few teachers.
- It requires no special aid or equipment.
- Children can be resources for each other through pair or group activities.
- Teacher can attend to children needing help.
- ALM allows the child to check his/her work against teachers.
- The beauty of the process is its simplicity.
- It allows room for all children's voices to be heard through discussion and presentation.

**Elements of ALM**

Students are involved in more than listening.

Less emphasis is placed on transmitting information.

Greater emphasis is on developments of student's skill.

Students are involved in high order thinking e.g. analysis, synthesis and evaluation.

Students, are engaged in activities e.g. reading, discussing and writing.

Greater emphasis is placed on students exploration of their own attitude and values.

**SUMMARY**

Syllabus is an outline and summary of topics to be covered in a course. Cultural syllabus, situational syllabus, structural or formal syllabus, task based syllabus, content based syllabus and lexical syllabus are the various types of syllabi. A language teaching syllabus involves combination of subject matter (what to teach) and linguistic matter (how to teach).

Method is a particular way of doing things. There are various methods of teaching English. They are grammar translation method, bilingual method, direct method and Dr. West's new method. Each method has its own characteristics or essential features, procedures, merits and limitations.

Approach is a way of dealing with things. There are various approaches to teach English. The important approaches are structural approach, situational approach, oral approach, structural oral situational approach, communicative approach and eclectic approach. Each approach has its own principles, procedure, merits and demerits.

Projects are special tasks assigned to students. Projects offer students challenging activities. Selection, planning, executing and evaluating are the various steps of project method. Students perform and evaluate their own work. It develops in students scientific attitude.

Action research is an action programme to find solution for a problem. It is a research undertaken by educational practitioners of local school to find solution for their problem. Steps in action research include locating a problem, analysing the cause of the problem, evolving a strategy to overcome the problem, applying the strategy, analysing the data and arriving at conclusions and generalisations.

Activity based learning is a new approach in teaching learning process. It refers to teaching through well designed and well developed cards. Procedure includes logos and milestones. Each milestone has various stages. For each language skill i.e. listening, speaking, reading and writing there are specific activities to be performed by the students.

Active learning methodology is based on the principle of learning by doing. It stresses active involvement in doing things. Reading, consolidating, constructing knowledge, mind mapping, making assessment, providing remedial instruction and summarising are the steps in active learning methodology. Reading, drawing a mind map, summarising, discussion and writing are the five basic skills emphasised in ALM.

# 7

# Tools of Evaluation

## EVALUATION

Evaluation is the process of gathering and interpreting evidence on changes in the behaviour of students as they progress through school. Evaluation refers to a series of activities that are designed to measure the effectiveness of teaching learning system as a whole. Evaluation is the collection, analysis and interpretation of information. It is an important component of teaching learning process. It helps teachers and learners to improve teaching learning. It is a continuous process and not a periodic exercise.

### Measurement

Measurement refers to the process finding the quantitative achievement of students in terms of scores. It is a process of measuring students' performance. Measurement is the collection and gathering of data e.g. students' score in an examination.

## CHARACTERISTICS OF A GOOD TEST

Test is a systematic procedure used to measure the performance, skill level, or knowledge of a learner on a specific subject matter. The following are the characteristics of a good test. They are: *(i)* objectivity; *(ii)* validity; *(iii)* reliability; *(iv)* feasibility; *(v)* administrability.

### Objectivity

Objectivity is being free from subjective judgement or pre suppositions. A good test is always free from subjective judgement.

## DIFFERENCE BETWEEN EVALUATION AND MEASUREMENT

There are marked differences between evaluation and measurement. They are summed up in the table given below:

| | Evaluation | Measurement |
|---|---|---|
| 1. | It is a modern concept. | It represents old traditional ideas. |
| 2. | Evaluation goes on with the process. | It is done at the end of the programme. |
| 3. | It is a continuous process. | It is not a continuous process. |
| 4. | It is an integral part of teaching learning process. | It is different from teaching learning process. |
| 5. | It is more reliable and valid. | It is not much reliable and valid. |
| 6. | There are greater changes of transfer in learning. | Change for the transfer is minimised. |
| 7. | Evaluation uses new scientific and up to date techniques. | Measurement uses dogmatic and unrealistic tools to measure attainment. |
| 8. | Evaluation is mostly internal. | Measurement is mostly external. |
| 9. | Evaluation is based on objectives of teaching. | Measurement is based on test scores. |
| 10. | Evaluation has more utilitarian value. The knowledge acquired is readily applied and made more useful. | Measurement has no utility in life. Its utility is limited only upto examination. It is never applied in life. |

### Validity

Validity refers to the appropriateness, meaningfulness and usefulness of the specific inferences made from scores. A test is said to be valid when it measures what it is supposed to measure.

### Types of Validity

There are five types of validity. They are content validity, criterion related validity, construct validity, face validity and factorial validity.

(a) **Content validity:** Content validity refers to coverage of course content and objectives specified. When an achievement test covers the course content and the objectives specified for the test, it is said to possess content validity.

(b) **Criterion related validity:** Criterion related validity refers to the extent to which test performance is related to some other valued measure of performance. Validity established on correlation with concurrent criterion yields concurrent validity and similarly, validity established against the scale of predictive criterion is called predictive validity.

(c) **Construct validity:** It is the validity based on the argument that a test is developed using a psychological or logical construct (idea). Test should provide evidence for measuring the construct.

(d) **Face validity:** Face validity refers to the acceptance of the apparent ability of a test to measure what it appears to measure. For example, a test to measure "skill in addition" should contain only items on addition.

(e) **Factorial validity:** It is the validity determined by a statistical technique known as factor analysis. It uses methods of explanation of inter correlations to identify factors constituting the test.

**Reliability**

Reliability refers to the accuracy and consistency with which a test measures what it is supposed to measure. A test that gives different results on different occasions is not reliable. There are two ways of looking at reliability. One is the comparability of measures provided by the different parts of the same test. The second is the comparability of measures provided by the test on different occasions.

**Administrability**

It refers to the actual giving of the test. The test should be easy to be administered. It means conducting the test properly.

**Feasibility**

It refers to the possibility of attending a test with an ability. A test should not be too hard or too easy.

**Characteristics of a Good English Test**

1. It must be objective, reliable, valid and feasible.

2. It should be based on aims and objectives in terms of language elements and skills.
3. A test should indicate the specific language items to be tested.
4. It should neither be too easy nor too difficult.
5. A good test should promote learning and encourage good teaching.
6. A good English test should test all language items.
7. Time and marking should be in proportion.
8. Due weightage should be given to knowledge of textbook, grammar, vocabulary and composition.
9. There should be a judicious combination of objective type questions, short answer questions and essay questions.
10. Test should be encouraging, not depressing.
11. A good English test should be area based and syllabus based.

## CONCEPT OF EVALUATION

Dr. Bloom believes that evaluation is a social and psychological activity. This is what an individual does whether he is buying a commodity or reading or writing and viewing a film. Evaluation has gone deep into human life.

According to NCERT evaluation is a continuous process. It forms an integral part of the total system of education and is intimately related to educational objectives. The questions of 'why' and 'what' relate to aims and objectives, while the questions of 'how' relate to learning experience and the questions of 'to what extent the learning experiences have brought about the required behavioural changes' relate to evaluation. This can be understood clearly by the triangle given below:

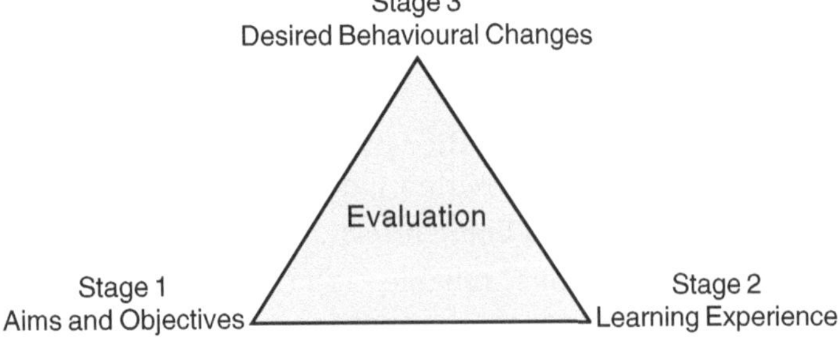

Evaluation enables us to measure the content as well as their interest and social behaviour, their way of thinking and doing things in life and their ability to adjust in social environment.

**Aims of Evaluation**

The following are the primary aims of evaluation. They are:

1. The primary aim of evaluation is to create antnimate relationship between the educational objectives and learning experiences.
2. It provides for remedial teaching.
3. It offers opportunity for learning activities.
4. It can guide and direct individuals in their educational and vocational pursuits.
5. It brings to light the strength and weakness of the student. It can help to reform curriculum.
6. It helps to know the taste, interest, aptitude, behaviour and social adjustment of the student.
7. Teachers ability and his success can also be adjudged.

**Types of Evaluation**

There are two types of evaluation, They are: *(i)* internal; and *(ii)* external.

1. **Internal evaluation:** Internal evaluation is the evaluation of the content side of achievement.
2. **External evaluation:** External evaluation refers to the evaluation of the physical fitness of pupils, their understanding, their interest, their aptitude, their behaviour and characteristics.

**Steps of Evaluation**

The following steps are followed in evaluation:

**Step 1:** Determining educational objectives.

**Step 2:** Organising learning experience to change the behaviour of pupils according to educational objectives.

**Step 3:** Measuring the behavioural changes or the objectives achieved.

**Tools or Devices of Evaluation**

The important tools of evaluation are: *(i)* observation device; *(ii)* interview; *(iii)* questionnaire; *(iv)* checklist; *(v)* pupils product; *(v)* records; *(vii)* rating scale; *(viii)* Geometric devices; *(ix)* cumulative record; *(x)* tests.

1. **Observation device**

Observation is essential to test the behaviour and qualities of pupils like truthfulness, cooperation, service mindedness etc. Observation is useful to evaluate group activities. Its main drawback is the subjectivity of the observers. This can be overcome by increasing the number of observers.

2. **Interview**

Interview is oral examination. It refers to meeting people for discussion. It is used in university exams at post graduate level. This helps to know the taste, aptitude, interest and sharpness of the intellect of the students.

3. **Questionnaire**

Questionnaire is a list of questions for obtaining information especially for statistical analysis. This may be written or oral. It helps to know the taste and attitude of the pupils.

4. **Checklist**

Checklist is another form of questionnaire. It is a list of specific statements with grade ABCD etc. Students should put a specific sign or tick mark to indicate to which they agree.

5. **Pupils product**

Pupils products are drawings or paintings, models or charts etc. They provide ample scope to judge the abilities and skills of the pupils. The products exhibit their entire personality.

6. **Records**

Diaries, anecdotal records and cumulative records are useful devices of evaluation. Diaries help us to know their taste, thoughts and problems. Cumulative records tell us the multifacious progress made by the students.

7. **Rating scale**

Rating scale is used to place in rank or class and to estimate a person with record to a specific behaviour for a considerable time.

8. **Geometric devices**

Geometry is a technique used to determine the mutual social relationship among the group members. This helps us to know the social stand of the students in the class.

9. **Cumulative records**

It is a comprehensive record. All information related to the students are registered in cumulative record. It gives the total picture of the child. Personal, physical, social, emotional, intellectual, academic and curricular information are recorded in it.

10. **Tests**

Test is a critical examination of a student's performance, knowledge and achievement. Tests can be oral or written. Written tests can be further classified into short answer type, essay type and objective type. Objective type tests include multiple choice test items, fill in the blanks test items, true or false test items and matching test items.

## CRITERION REFERENCED AND NORM REFERENCED TESTS

### Criterion Referenced Test

Criterion referenced tests are the tests designed to provide information on specific knowledge or skills possessed by a student. These tests usually cover small units of content and are closely related to instruction. It is used to identify a students' specific strength and weakness in relation to skills defined as the goals of instruction but it does not compare a student with others.

### Norm Referenced Test

Norm referenced tests are the tests designed to measure how a student's performance compares with that of other students. Most of the standardised achievement tests are norm referenced tests.

### Difference Between Criterion and Norm Referenced Tests

There are marked differences between criterion referenced and norm referenced tests. They are enumerated in the table given below.

| Criterion Referenced Tests | Norms Referenced Tests |
|---|---|
| 1. It is used to determine which of the specified objectives of instruction a particular student has attained. | It is used to determine how much overall knowledge of some subject a particular student has achieved. |
| 2. The excellence or deficiency of a student's achievement is judged by the attainment of objectives by the student. | The excellence or deficiency of a student's achievement is judged by his stand among those in the group. |
| 3. The items in a criterion referenced test cluster around a limited number of specific objectives. | The items in norm referenced tests are diffused more widely across the domain of learning. |
| 4. Criterion referenced tests indicate that certain things will be learned. | Norm referenced test scores indicate a student's degree of success in learning. |
| 5. Criterion referenced test is useful to take categorical pass fail decisions. | Norm referenced test is useful to measure a person's level of knowledge and understanding. |

### Summative and Formative Tests

In teaching learning process we have to make both formative evaluation and summative evaluation. We use formative tests and summative tests to make these evaluations.

**Formative tests:** These are the tests administered during units of instruction that measure progress and guide the content and pace of the lesson. These are the tests used for midcourse evaluation. Formative evaluation is an integral part of teaching learning process. This is used to monitor teaching learning process during instruction and to provide continuous feedback both to pupils and teachers concerning learning success and failures. Feedback facilitates successful learning and identifies errors to be corrected.

**Summative tests:** Summative evaluation is assessment that follows instruction and evaluates students' knowledge and skill. Summative tests are administered at the end of course instruction. These are the tests designed to determine the extent to which instructional objectives have been achieved and used for assigning grades. Summative tests diagnose both positive and negative aspects of the overall programme and finds reasons for them at the end of the programme.

**A comparative study of formative and summative evaluation**

| Factor | Formative Evaluation | Summative Evaluation |
|---|---|---|
| 1. Time | During instruction | At the end of a course |
| 2. Emphasis | Mostly cognitive | Generally cognitive, sometimes psychomotor, occasionally affective |
| 3. Instrument | Specially designed by the teacher (quiz or test) | Final examination |
| 4. Objective | Specific to the unit | Whole course objectives |
| 5. Item difficulty | can not be specified | Average difficulty ranging from 35% to 75% with some easy and some difficult items |
| 6. Scoring | Criterion-referenced | Generally norm-referenced |
| 7. Method of reporting scores | Individual pattern of pass/fail scores | Total score |
| 8. Function | Feed back to students and teachers | Assigning grades |

**Different Types of Tests**

A test is a procedure for measuring ability, knowledge or performance developed during a course of learning. It is a device to reinforce learning and motivate students. Tests provide feedback to students indicating their strengths and weaknesses.

There are different types of tests. They are: *(i)* achievement test; *(ii)* standardised achievement test; *(iii)* aptitude test; *(iv)* proficiency test; *(v)* diagnostic test.

1. **Achievement test:** Achievement tests are the tests designed to provide a general survey of students' academic attainments, knowledge, understanding and mastery in a given subject after a certain period of instruction. The quality as well as the quantity attained

in the subject is measured by achievement test. The result of the achievement test is required for promotion of a student to the next higher grade.

Achievement tests are of two types. They are: *(i)* classroom or teacher made achievement tests; *(ii)* standardised achievement test.

*(i)* **Classroom or teacher made achievement test:** This category includes oral tests, written tests, spelling tests, reading tests and arithmetic tests. Written test includes objective types tests, short answer questions, paragraph questions and essay questions. They help to measure the achievement of the students but generalisation is not possible.

*(ii)* **Standardised achievement test:** Standardised achievement test is a test which gives similar results when employed by different people. Standardised test is a form of measurement normed against a specific population. Standardisation refers to the process of analysing the essential steps in a skill or activity to determine the most efficient and safe way of performing it. These tests are wide in scope. These are prepared by national level experts. They cover wider population. Different examiners give approximately the same score to the same children when the test is administered to them.

3. **Aptitude test:** Aptitude test is a test that measures a student's inclination for learning or performing a job. Aptitude test is a device or technique designed to indicate a person's potential ability for performing a specific activity. Most of the entrance tests and competitive examinations are based on the concept of aptitude. Verbal aptitude, musical aptitude, numerical aptitude, special aptitude and language aptitude tests are the common aptitude tests.

4. **Proficiency test:** Proficiency test is a test that measures the achievement of the students in a specific task which they will be required later to perform. While the achievement test is based on the course of study,

proficiency test is based on the general understanding of the subject concerned. Communicative skills are tested by proficiency test. Proficiency tests are designed to assess the ability of students in applying their knowledge to real life situations.

5. **Diagnostic test:** Diagnostic test is a test used to diagnose or analyse, that is to locate an individual's specific areas of weakness or strength and to suggest the possible causes. These tests enable the teachers to identify the problem areas in the teaching learning process and to plan the remedial work suitably. These tests are mostly used to test reading comprehension, rate of learning, vocabulary and paragraph and sentence comprehension.

**TYPES OF ACHIEVEMENTTEST**

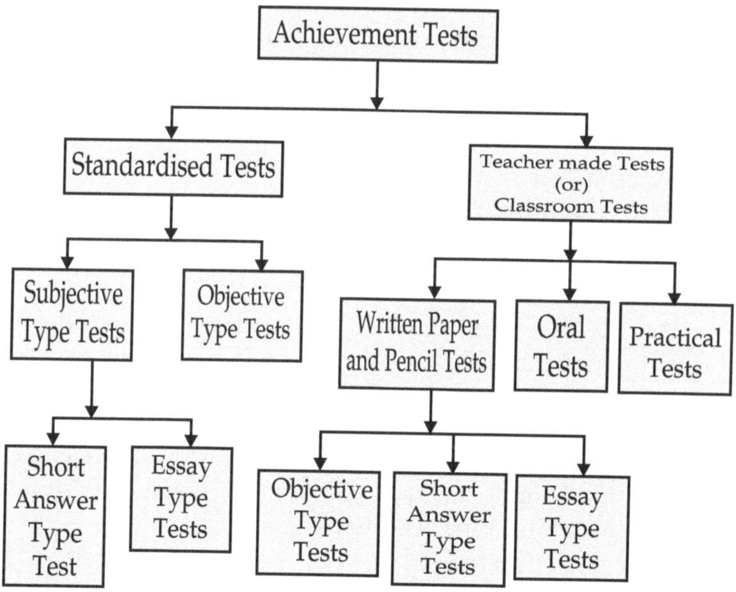


**Teacher made Tests**

These tests are designed by the teachers for the purpose of conducting classroom tests. These teacher made tests can be in the form of oral and written tests. These tests have a limited area of application and are prepared almost by all teachers according to their requirements. Teacher made oral tests are designed to measure the students' skills in listening and speaking. Written tests are designed to test the level of students knowledge, comprehension and written expression. Unit tests and terminal examinations come under this category.

**Oral Test**

Oral test is a test administered orally. It is mostly used in lower classes. It plays an important role in testing students' listening and speaking skills. Oral test is used to test the following listening skills in students: *(i)* pronunciation in reading and fluency; *(ii)* comprehension; and *(iii)* expression.

1. Reading includes stress, pause, intonation, pronunciation and fluency.
2. Comprehension includes auditory comprehension, reading comprehension, picture comprehension and story comprehension.
3. Expression includes ability to report, ability to express and ability to converse.

**Types of Oral Test**

There are two types of oral test. They are continuous assessment test and short oral tests.

## OBJECTIVETYPETESTS

Objective tests are the tests that measure the students' ability to remember facts and figures. These tests are free from personal feelings or presuppositions. Objectives type test items require brief and precise answer. The following are the important objective type test items. *(i)* Multiple choice test item; *(ii)* Completion type test item; *(iii)* true or false test item; *(iv)* matching type test items.

**Multiple Choice Test Items**

Multiple choice test items are the most widely used objective type test items. This is a question with four choices for answer. The question part is called stem. Choices from which correct answer is to be chosen are called alternatives. Out of the four alternatives one is the correct answer and the others are distractors.

e.g. There are —— vowel sounds in English. (a) 8 (b) 12 (c) 20 (d) 26

**Completion Type Test Items**

These are test items with incomplete statements and blanks. Students should fill in the blanks with suitable word or phrase. e.g. There are twelve —— vowels in English.

**True or False Test Items**

True or false test items are the statements which the students should specify whether true or false. e.g. There are forty four sounds in English. True/false.

**Matching Test Items**

Matching type questions contain two sets of items given in two columns. Students have to match the item from one set with an item from the other set. The number of words in the second column may be more than the words in the first column.

| Column A | Column B |
|---|---|
| Pure vowels | 8 |
| Gliding vowels | 12 |
| English alphabets | 24 |
| Total sounds | 26 |
| Consonants | 44 |
| | 40 |

## WRITTENTESTS

Written tests are otherwise called paper pencil tests. The written tests are classified into two categories namely: *(i)* subjective type tests; and *(ii)* Objective type of tests. Subjective type tests are meant for testing the productive skills of the students. Objective type tests are meant for testing the ability of the students to remember facts and figures. Objective type tests are suitable for lower class. Subjective type tests are suitable for higher classes.

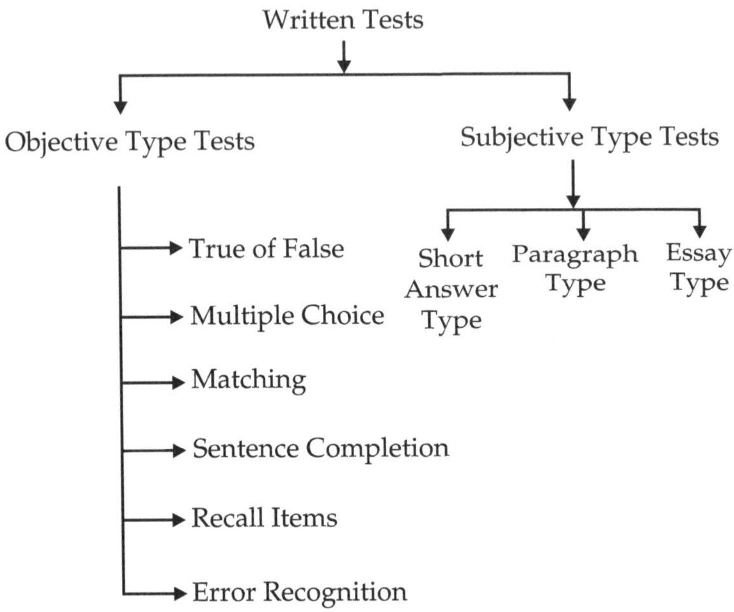


**Subjective Type tests**

Subjective type tests are meant for testing the productive skill of the students. These tests demand free responses from the students. These tests consist of open ended questions. Answers are descriptive in nature. Subjective type tests include: *(i)* short answer type question; *(ii)* paragraph question; and *(iii)* essay type question.

**1. Short answer type question**

These tests/questions are thought provoking. The content and educational objectives are tested in this testing. The questions help to test the achievement of the students relating to a particular concept. Answer should be provided in two or three sentences.

**2. Paragraph type question**

These test items require the students to generate ideas regarding the topic they intend to write on. Paragraph contains a number of sentences grouped together which are related to the given topic. A good paragraph should have a topic and topic sentence. It should have logically connected sequencing of sentences. It should have coherence. It should be neither long nor short.

**3. Essay type question**

These are the questions/tests that demand long answers. It is the most popular form of written examination to measure the achievement of students. These tests bring to light the mastery of language skills like organisation, development and consolidation of ideas. These tests provide opportunities to students to do independent and original thinking and to express themselves freely.

## CONSTRUCTION OF A GOOD TEST

Tests are of different kinds – achievement tests, diagnostic tests, personality tests, intelligence tests, aptitude tests etc. We have tests of different aspects of academic achievement too, such as spelling tests, reading tests, arithmetic tests etc. Not only researchers but class teachers too make use of them. But the tests used by these two categories of people are not of the same kind – the former use what are known as standardized tests and the latter, use class room tests or teacher made tests. Classroom tests have no place in research. They are useful only to teachers and administrators. They help to measure the achievement of pupils but generalisation is not possible. Construction of an achievement test is a serious job for a teacher. It requires adequate planning before hand. It has the following steps.

**Step 1: Setting Objectives**

A clear objective of planning is important to frame a test. The objectives must be defined in terms of specific behaviour changes expected in the pupils after achieving a course or a standard.

**Steps 2: Coverage of syllabus or contents**

A good test should cover all the major units and sub topics. No major unit should be left out. There must be a reasonable coverage of various aspects of learning experiences.

**Step 3: Decision about the types of items/questions**

Decision about the types of questions to be set in the test paper is also an essential aspect of its construction. As pointed out earlier, all the three forms i.e. Essay type, short answer type and objective type should find place in a good achievement test.

**Step 4: Decision about the time**

The total time given to the students for giving responses to the items of test should also be decided.

**Step 5: Preparation of blue print**

Preparation of blue print is essential for construction of a good test. Blue print is the design of the paper. It shows distribution of questionwise marks covering specific objectives and topics. It lists out forms and weightage of questions. The difficulty value and discriminating power of the test items are calculated.

**Step 6: Preparation of scoring key and marking scheme**

To ensure objectivity in scoring, scoring key is prepared. Scoring Key must be prepared not only for objective type test items but also for short answer, paragraph and essay type questions. Scoring procedure also should be determined.

**Preparation of a blue print**

Blue print is the design of the test. It is to be prepared in advance. We should discuss the blue prints with as many experts as possible. Blue print distinguishes a standardised test from a class test or teacher made test.

**Essential of Blue Print**

Perfection of a blue print depends on:

1. The coverage of course content
2. The coverage of course objectives
3. Determination of the types of questions
4. Determination of weightage of questions in terms of mark allotment.

**Steps in Preparation of Blue Print**

1. Determining relative weightage to different areas like objectives, items to content and types of questions.
2. Determining itemwise and content wise distribution of marks.
3. Assembling the test items conforming to the blue print.

4. Writing scoring key and marking scheme.
5. Finally making questionwise analysis to assess the test for imbalance or defects.

A model design of the blue print is given below. These procedures may be followed in constructing test for terminal or annual examinations.

**Design**

| Subject: English | | | Time: 30 minutes |
|---|---|---|---|
| Unit: Conditional Sentences | | | Maximum marks: 25 |
| Class: X | | | Date : ........................ |
| **(a)** | **Weightage to objectives** | | **Marks/Percentage** |
| 1. | Knowledge of structure | | 6 or 24% (25) |
| 2. | Skill of reading | | 7 or 28% (25) |
| 3. | Skill of writing | | 12 or 48% (50) |
| **(b)** | **Weightage to content** | | **Marks** |
| 1. | Conditional clause | | 1 |
| 2. | Transposition of clauses | | 2 |
| 3. | Sequence of Tenses | | 7 |
| 4. | Inversion | | 2 |
| 5. | Conjunctions | | 3 |
| 6. | Use of will and shall | | 2 |
| 7. | Factual condition (type 1) | | 2 |
| 8. | Imaginary condition (type 2) | | 4 |
| 9. | Unfulfilled condition past (type 3) | | 2 |
| | Total | | 25 |
| **(c)** | **Weightage to question types** | | **Marks** |
| 1. | Objective Type | – | 13 marks or 52% |
| 2. | Short answer type | – | 12 marks or 48% |
| | | | 25 marks or 100% |

**Tools of Evaluation**

| Objectives | Knowledge | | Skills | | | | Total |
|---|---|---|---|---|---|---|---|
| Content | Vocabulary | Structure | Listening | Speaking | Reading | Writing | |
| Conditional clause | | 1(1) | | | | | 1(1) |
| Transposition of clause | | 1(1) | | | 1(1) | | 2(1) |
| Sequence of Tenses | | 3(1) | | | 4(2) | | 7(3) |
| Inversion of subject and verb | | | | | 2(2) | | 2(2) |
| Conjunctions | | 1(1) | | | 2(2) | | 3(3) |
| Use of will and shall | | | | 2(1) | | | 2(2) |
| Structure Type 1 | | | | 1(1) | 1(1) | | 2(2) |
| Structure Type 2 | | | | | 2(2) | 2(2) | 4(4) |
| Structure Type 3 | | | | | 1(1) | 1(1) | 2(2) |
| Total | | 6(4) | | 3(3) | 13(11) | 3(3) | 25(21) |

In this way every question item of a question paper is analysed separately

**Scoring Key and Marking Scheme**

Scoring key should be prepared for multiple choice and other objective type questions in the paper. This helps the examiner to value the answer scripts effectively. In the scoring key, allotted marks are posted in the marks column.

**Scoring Key**

| Question No. | Answer | Marks |
|---|---|---|
| | Total Marks | |

Further, the teacher should prepare 'marking scheme' for essay type and short answer type questions providing the division of mark for different aspects of the expected answers.

### Marking Scheme

In the marking scheme, the short answer type questions and essay questions are marked.

| Question No | Answer | Marks |
|---|---|---|
| SECTION II | | |
| Short answers | | |
| 1. | | |
| 2. | | |
| 3. | | |
| 4. | | |
| 5. | | |
| SECTION III | | |
| Essay answers | | |
| 1. | | |
| 2. | | |
| 3. | | |
| | Total Marks | |

## PILOT STUDY

After finalising blue print, we have to construct the test items. The first drafts is subjected to 'try out' or pilot study. It is administered to a small sample of the population for whom it is intended. Pilot study is essential to refine the test items.

### Item Analysis

Item analysis refers to an elaborate set of statistical procedure to make scientific scrutiny and critical judgement of the included test items. In the item analysis, the difficulty level of the test items and the discriminating power of the test items are determined in order to make decision regarding inclusion or deletion.

### Item Difficulty

Test item difficulty refers to the percentage of students who answer the given test item correctly. The level of difficulty is determined by using the formula:

$P = (Nr/Nt) \times 100$

Where

P – percentage of students who answer the test item correctly.

Nr – number of students who answer the test item correctly.

Nt – total number of students who attempt to answer the test item.

On the basis of this analysis, too easy and too difficult test items are deleted in the final form of achievement test.

**Item Discriminating Power**

A test item is said to possess adequate discriminating power when it is capable of differentiating between superior and inferior students. To determine item discriminating power, the following simple formula is used even though there are many different computational schemes.

$D = (U - L)/N$

D = index of item discriminating power

U = Number of students in the upper group who answer the test items correctly (usually 27% of the total group)

L = Number of students in the lower group who answer the test items correctly (usually 27% of the total group)

N = Number of students in each group

After item analysis, too easy and too difficult test items and the test items that fail to discriminate are deleted. Then the final form of the achievement test is administered to larger samples and norms are calculated for the purpose of comparison. Norms may be defined as the average performance obtained by a sample group that took the test during its standardisation period at different levels. For each grade or age the average score becomes the norm.

## CHARACTERISTICS OF A STANDARDISED TEST

1. Standardised tests are based on the content and objectives of teaching common to many schools.
2. Not just one, but a team of experts are involved in the writing of test items.

3. Item analysis is done on the basis of a pilot study, unlike in the case of a class room test.
4. Norms are calculated for the purpose of comparison between grades, schools, age levels and sexes.
5. They cover large segments of knowledge and skills.
6. Test manuals are prepared.
7. Fairly a large sample, not just one class is involved in the standardisation of the test.

## SUMMARY

Measurement refers to the process of finding the quantitative achievement of the students in terms of scores. Evaluation is the process of gathering and interpreting evidence on changes in the behaviour of students as they progress through school. There are some marked differences between measurement and evaluation.

Objectivity, validity, reliability, administrability and feasibility are the characteristics of a good test. In addition to the above characteristics, a good English test includes language elements and skills and adequate coverage of grammar, vocabulary and composition.

There are two types of evaluation: internal evaluation and external evaluation. Evaluation consists of three steps such as determining educational objectives, organising learning experience to change the behaviour of pupils according to educational needs and measuring the behavioural changes for the objective achieved

The important tools or devices of evaluation are observation, interview, questionnaire checklist, pupils' product, records, rating scale, geometric devices, cumulative records and tests. Each tool has its own context, procedure and application.

Criterion referenced tests are the tests designed to provide information on specific knowledge or skills possessed by a student. Norm referenced tests are the tests designed to measure how a student's performance compares with that of other students. There are marked differences between these two types of tests.

Formative evaluation is midcourse evaluation and criterion referenced. It provides feedback to students and teachers. Summative evaluation is the evaluation done at the end of the course and it is generally norm referenced. It is widely used for assigning grades.

A test is a procedure for measuring ability, knowledge or performance developed during a course of learning. It is a device to reinforce learning and motivate students. There are different types of test: achievement test, standardised achievement test, aptitude test, proficiency test and diagnostic tests.

Achievement tests can be classified as teacher made tests and standarised tests. Tests make use of objective type test items and subjective type test items. Objective type test items are multiple choice test item, completion type test item, true or false test item and matching test item. Subjective type test items include short answer question, paragraph question and essay question.

Construction of a good standardised test includes various steps such as setting objectives, coverage of syllabus, decision about type of test items, deciding time, preparation of blue print, preparation of scoring key and marking scheme, pilot study, item analysis and finalising the final form the test. Norms are calculated for the purpose of comparison between grades, schools, age levels and sexes.

# 8

# Educational Statistics

## MEANING OF STATISTICS

Statistics is a body of mathematical techniques or processes for gathering, organising, analysing, and interpreting numerical data. Because most research yields such quantitative data, statistics is a basic tool of measurement, evaluation, and research. The word statistics is sometimes used to describe the numerical data gathered. Statistical data describe group behaviour or group characteristics abstracted from a number of individual observations that are combined to make generalisations possible. In simple words, statistics is representation of any data. It is a science of explaining the data in systematic manner. Statistics deals with quantification of data.

## TWO TYPES OF DATA

There are two types of recognised data in the application of statistical treatments. They are: *(i)* parametric data; and *(ii)* non parametric data.

### Parametric Data

Parametric data are measured data and parametric statistical tests assume that the data are normally, or nearly normally, distributed. Parametric tests are applied to both interval and ratio scaled data.

### Non Parametric Data

Non parametric data are either counted (nominal) or ranked (ordinal). Nonparametric tests, sometimes known as distribution-free tests, do not rest on the more stringent assumption of normally distributed populations.

## TWO TYPES OF ANALYSIS

Two types of statistical application are relevant. They are: *(i)* descriptive analysis; and *(ii)* inferential analysis.

### Descriptive Analysis

Descriptive statistical analysis limits generalisation to the particular group of individuals observed. No conclusions are extended beyond this group, and any similarity to those outside the group cannot be assumed. The data describe one group and that group only. Much simple action research involves descriptive analysis and provides valuable information about the nature of a particular group of individuals.

### Inferential Analysis

Inferential statistical analysis always involves the process of sampling and the selection of a small group assumed to be related to the population from which it is drawn. The small group is known as the sample, and the large group is the population. Drawing conclusions about populations based on observations of samples is the purpose of inferential analysis.

## STATISTICAL MEASURES

Several basic types of statistical measures are appropriate in describing and analysing data in a meaningful way: They are:

(i) Measures of central tendency or averages
    Mean
    Median
    Mode

(ii) Measures of spread or dispersion
    Range
    Variance
    Standard deviation

(iii) Measures of relative position
    Standard scores
    Percentile rank
    Percentile score

(iv) Measures of relationship

Coefficient of correlation

**Measures of Central Tendency**

Nonstatisticians use averages to describe the characteristics of groups in a general way. But to the statistician the term average is unsatisfactory, for there are a number of types of averages. Of the many averages that may be used, three have been selected as most useful in educational research: the mean, the median, and the mode.

Mean ($\bar{X}$)

The mean of a distribution is commonly understood as the arithmetic average. The term grade-point average, familiar to students, is a mean value. It is computed by dividing the sum of all the scores by the number of scores. In formula form

where X = mean

$$\bar{X} = \frac{\Sigma x}{N}$$

Σ = Sum of

X = Scores in a distribution

N = Number of scores

Example

| | X |
|---|---|
| | 7 |
| | 6 |
| | 5 |
| | 4 |
| | 3 |
| | 2 |
| ΣX | 27 |
| N = | 6 |
| X = | 27/6 = 4.50 |

The mean is probably the most useful of all statistical measures, for, in addition to the information that it provides, it is the base from which many other important measures are computed.

**Different computations of mean**

We use different formulas for ungrouped date and grouped data. They are:

(i) Mean = $\frac{\sum x}{N}$ useful for ungrouped data

(ii) Mean = $\frac{\sum fx}{N}$ useful for grouped data

(iii) $M = Am + \frac{\sum fx}{N} \times i$

**Application of formula 1 (ungrouped data)**

| Ungrouped data | |
|---|---|
| 14 | 41 |
| 23 | 32 |
| 32 | 41 |
| 17 | 37 |
| 18 | 18 |
| 15 | 16 |
| 16 | 40 |
| 12 | 32 |
| 21 | 18 |
| 18 | |
| 19 | |

Mean = $\frac{\sum x}{N} = \frac{480}{20} = 24$

**Application of formula 2**

| | | x | f | fx |
|---|---|---|---|---|
| 12 | 19 | 12 | 1 | 12 |
| 14 | 21 | 14 | 1 | 14 |
| 15 | 23 | 15 | 1 | 15 |
| 16 | 32 | 16 | 2 | 32 |
| 16 | 32 | 17 | 1 | 17 |
| 17 | 32 | 18 | 4 | 72 |
| 18 | 37 | 19 | 1 | 19 |
| 18 | 40 | 21 | 1 | 21 |
| 18 | 41 | 23 | 1 | 23 |
| 18 | 41 | 32 | 3 | 96 |
| | | 37 | 1 | 37 |
| | | 40 | 1 | 40 |
| | | 41 | 2 | 82 |
| | | | | 480 |

$$\text{Mean} = \frac{\sum x}{N} = \frac{480}{20} = 24$$

**Application of formula 3**

X – raw score of real score

x – midpoint

less scores – more intervals for accuracy

$$\text{Mean} = \pm\frac{\sum x}{N} \times \text{i}$$

| C.I | Mid pint | f | x | fx |
|---|---|---|---|---|
| 11 - 15 | 13 | 3 | -4 | -12 |
| 16 - 20 | 18 | 8 | -3 | -24 |
| 21 - 25 | 23 | 2 | -2 | -4 |
| 26 - 30 | 28 | 0 | -1 | 0 |
| 31 - 35 | 33 | 3 | 0 | 0 |
| 36 - 40 | 38 | 2 | +1 | +2 |
| 41 - 45 | 43 | 2 | +2 | +4 |
| | | | | -34 |

$$\bar{X}\text{(mean)} = \text{Am} \pm \frac{\sum fx}{N} \times \text{i} = 33 - \frac{-34 \times 5}{20} 8.5 = 33 - 8.5 = 24.5$$

Mean = 24.5

| C.I | Mid pint | f | x | fx |
|---|---|---|---|---|
| 11 - 20 | 15.5 | 11 | -3 | -33 |
| 21 - 30 | 25.5 | 2 | -2 | -4 |
| 31 - 40 | 35.5 | 5 | -1 | -5 |
| 41 - 50 | 45.5 | 2 | 0 | 0 |
| | | | Σfx | -42 |

$$\text{Mean} = \text{A.M} \pm \frac{\sum fx}{N} \times \text{i} = 45.5 - \frac{42}{20} \times 10 = 45.5 - 21 = 24.5$$

**Median**

The median is a point (not necessarily a score) in an array, above and below which one-half of the scores fall. It is a measure of position rather than of magnitude and is frequently found by inspection rather than by calculation. When there are an odd number of united scores, the median is the middle score, as in the example below:

7 3 scores above
6
5
4 median
3
2 3 scores below
1

One purpose of the mean and the median is to represent the "typical" score; most of the time it is satisfactory to use the mean for this purpose. However, when the distribution of scores is such that most scores are at one end and relatively few are at the other (known as a skewed distribution), the median is preferable because it is not influenced by extreme scores at either end of the distribution.

**Computation of the Median for Grouped Data**

If the data are available in the form of frequency distribution, we can calculate the median as given.

| Scores | f |
|---|---|
| 65 - 69 | 1 |
| 60 - 64 | 3 |
| 55 - 59 | 4 |
| 50 - 54 | 7 |
| 45 - 49 | 9 |
| 40 - 44 | 11 |
| 35 - 39 | 8 |
| 30 - 34 | 4 |
| 25 - 29 | 2 |
| 20 - 24 | 1 |
| | N = 50 |

i = class interval

N = Total of all the frequencies

Median table.

| Class Interval | Continuous Class Interval | frequency (f) | Cumulative (f) frequency |
|---|---|---|---|
| 65 - 69 | 64.5 - 69.5 | 1 | 50 |
| 60 - 64 | 59.5 - 64.5 | 3 | 49 |
| 55 - 59 | 54.5 - 59.5 | 4 | 46 |
| 50 - 54 | 49.5 - 54.5 | 7 | 42 |
| 45 - 49 | 44.5 - 49.5 | 9 | 35 |
| 40 - 44 | 39.5 - 44.5 | 11 | 26 |
| 35 - 39 | 34.5 - 39.5 | 8 | 15 |
| 30 - 34 | 29.5 - 34.5 | 4 | 7 |
| 25 - 29 | 24.5 - 29.5 | 2 | 3 |
| 20 - 24 | 19.5 - 24.5 | 1 | 1 |

1. To calculate median continuous class interval is necessary. For example, in between the class intervals 20 - 24 and 25 - 29 continuation is missing. That is the points 24.1, 24.2, 24.3, 24.4, 24.5 ...... 24.9 are missing. Hence class intervals should be mentioned with their real limits. To have the real limits 0.5 should be reduced from the lower

class limit and 0.5 is added with the upper class limit. In this way continuous class intervals or real limits of the scores are located.

2. To calculate cumulative frequency (F) frequency distributions are added from the ascending order. Thus in the median table cumulative frequency and the continuous class intervals are located.

   L = Lower limit of the median class interval

   Which is 39,5

   N = number of students = 50

   F = cumulative frequency before the median class = 15

   i = class interval = 5

$$= 39.5 + \left( \frac{50/2 - 15}{11} \right) \times 5$$

$$= 39.5 + \frac{10}{11} \times 5 = 39.5 + 4.5 = 44$$

**Mode**

The mode is the score that occurs most frequently in a distribution. It is located by inspection rather than by computation. In grouped data distributions, the mode is assumed to be the midscore of the interval in which the greatest frequency occurs.

6
5
4 ⎫
  ⎬ Mode
4 ⎭
3
2
1

In some distributions there may be more than one mode. A two-mode distribution is referred to as bimodal, more than two, multimodal.

### Computation of Mode

Mode can be computed for grouped data as well as ungrouped data as shown below.

**(a) In case of ungrouped data**

In case of ungrouped data, mode can be easily computed merely by looking at it. All that one has to do is to find out the score which is repeated maximum number of times.

Example. Suppose we have to find out the value of the mode from the following scores of the students.

25, 29, 24, 25, 27, 25, 28, 25, 29

Here the score 25 is repeated maximum number of times and thus value of the mode in this case is 25.

**(b) In case of grouped data.**

In the case where data are available in the form of a frequency distribution, the mode is computed from the following formula:

Mode ($M_o$) = 3 $M_d$ – 2 M where $M_d$ is the median and $M_1$ the mean of the given distribution.

In this way for the computation of mode in the case of frequency distribution, first of all mean as well as median of the distribution is computed and then with the help of the above formula Mode is calculated. For illustration we can take the distribution previously given. We know the mean and median of this distribution. Now we can use these results for the computation of the mode.

$M_d$ = 44.05 M = 44.6

Therefore, $M_o$ = 3 × 44.05 – 2 × 44.6

= 132.15 – 89.2

= 42.95

### When to use Mean, Median and Mode

A mere knowledge of mean, median and mode won't do. An adequate knowledge of when to use mean, when to use median and when to use mode is very important.

### When to Use Mean

1. Mean is the most reliable accurate measure of the central tendency of a distribution in comparison to median and mode

in the case where a reliable and accurate measure of central tendency is needed, we compute mean for the given data.

2. Mean can be given an algebraic treatment and is better, suited to further arithmetical computation. It can be easily employed for the computation of various statistics like Standard Deviation, Coefficient of correlation etc.
3. It is not proper to compute mean for the series that have extreme items. It should be calculated only when the series has no extreme items and each score carries equal weight in, determining the central tendency.

**When to use Median**

1. Median is the exact mid point of a series as 50% cases lie below and above it. Therefore, when the exact mid-point of the distribution is desired, median is to be computed.
2. Median is not affected by the extreme scores in the series. Therefore, when a series contains extreme scores, the median is perhaps the most representative central measure.
3. In case of an open ended distribution (incomplete distribution "BC and above" or "20 and below" etc.) mean is impossible to be calculated. In such cases, median is the most reliable measure that can be computed.
4. Mean cannot be calculated graphically. But in case of median we can compute it graphically. Therefore, when we have suitable graphs like frequency curve, polygon etc. we should try to compute median.
5. The median is specifically useful for the data the items of which cannot precisely be measured quantitatively e.g. qualities like health, culture, honesty, intelligence. etc.

**When to use the mode**

1. Therefore, in cases where a quick and approximate measure of central tendency is all that is desired, we compute mode.
2. Mode is that value of the item which occurs most frequently or is repeated maximum number of times in a given series. Therefore, when we need to know the most often recurring score or value of the item in a series, we compute mode.

3. Mode can be computed from the histogram and other frequency curve. Therefore, when we already have a graphical representation of the distribution in the form of such figures, it is appropriate to compute mode instead of mean.

**Measures of Dispersion**

Measures of central tendency provide insufficient base for the comparison of two or more frequency distributions or sets of scores. So there is a great need for measures of variability or disperson. There are chiefly four measures of spread or dispersion such as: *(i)* the range; *(ii)* the quartile deviation (Q) the average deviation AD; *(iii)* the average deviation (AD) and *(iv)* standard deviation. Each of the above measures of variability gives us the degree of variability or dispersion by the use of a single number and tells us how the individual scores are scattered or spread over throughout the distribution or given data.

**1. Range (R)**

The range, the simplest measure of dispersion, is the difference between the highest and lowest scores. For reading scores the range is 40 (95 - 55). For arithmetic scores the range is 8 (79 - 71). Range is the indicator of variability and is easily calculated. It takes into account only the extremes and ignores others. It is the simplest measure of dispersions which gives us a rough estimate of the spreadness of scores.

**2. The Quartile Deviation (Q)**

It is computed by the formula $Q = \frac{Q_1 \text{ and } Q_3}{2}$ where $Q_1$ and $Q_3$ represent the 1st and 3rd Quartiles of the distribution under consideration The amount $Q_3$ and Q1 is nothing but the difference or range between 3rd and 1st Quartile. It is designated as the inter quartile range. For computing Quartile Deviation, this interquartile range is divided by 2 and therefore, Quartile Deviation is also named as semi-interquartile range. In this way for computing Q, the values of $Q_1$ and $Q_3$ are first determined and then by applying the above formula we try to get the value of Quartile Deviation.

### 3. The average deviation (AD)

"Average Deviation or AD" is the mean of the deviations of all the separate scores in the series taken from their mean (occasionally from the median or mode.)" It is the simplest measure of variability that takes into account the fluctuation or variation of all the items in a series.

**Computation of average deviation (A.D.) from ungrouped data.**

To calculate the quartile Deviation Q1, the value of $\frac{N}{4}$ is needed. To know Q3 the value of $\frac{3N}{4}$ is needed.

The method applied to calculate median is used to know Q1 and Q3.

$$Q1 = L + \frac{\left[\frac{N}{4} - F\right]}{f} \times i$$

$$Q3 = L + \frac{\left[\frac{3N}{4} - F\right]}{f} \times i$$

L = Lower limit of the median class interval

N = Number of students

F = Cumulative frequency before the median class

i = Class interval

f = Frequency

### 4. Standard Deviation

The standard deviation is the square root of the variance. It is most frequently used as a measure of spread or dispersion of scores in a distribution. Standard Deviation is more accurate than the average deviation. To calculate standard deviation, individual deviations must be obtained. Then the individual deviations are squared and added. The sum of the squared deviation is divided by the strength of the class N. The quotient should have square root and this is standard deviation. This is mentioned by the symbol σ (sigma).

$$\sigma = \sqrt{\frac{\Sigma x^2}{N}}$$

The above formula is used if the strength is minimum. If the frequency is high, the following formula is used

$$\sigma = \sqrt{\frac{\Sigma fd^2}{N} - \left[\frac{\Sigma fd^2}{N}\right]} \times i$$

**Computation of SD**

The following example illustrates how standard deviation can be computed.

| CI | f | x | fx | fx² |
|---|---|---|---|---|
| 11 - 20 | 1 | -3 | -3 | +9 |
| 21 - 30 | 1 | -2 | -2 | +4 |
| 31 - 40 | 1 | -1 | -1 | +1 |
| 41 - 50 | 3 | 0 | 0 | 0 |
| 51 - 60 | 3 | +1 | +3 | +3 |
| 61 - 70 | 7 | +2 | +4 | +28 |
| 71 - 80 | 1 | +3 | +3 | +9 |
| 81 - 90 | 3 | +4 | +12 | +48 |
| | | | | 102 |

N = 20

$\Sigma fx = 32 - 6 = 26$

$\Sigma fx^2 = 102$

$$\left(\frac{\Sigma fx}{N}\right)^2 = \left(\frac{26}{20}\right)^2 = \frac{676}{400} = 1.69$$

$$\text{S.D.} = i\sqrt{\frac{\sum fx^2}{N} - \left(\frac{\sum fx}{N}\right)^2}$$

$$= 10\sqrt{\frac{\sum fx^2}{N} - 1.69}$$

$$= 10 \times \sqrt{5.1 - 1.69}$$

$$= 10 \times \sqrt{3.41}$$

$$= 10 \times 1.84 = 18.4$$

**The Normal Probability Curve**

If the scores are most numerous in the middle, (2) and the scores grow less and less common away from the mean and (3) the scores frequencies decline symmetrically on both sides of the middle, we will get a bell shaped curve. Bell shaped curve is obtained if N increases, and the smooth distribution is called Gaussian curve. The probability of a given event is defined as the expected frequency of occurrence of this even among events of a like sort". We should keep in mind that "the normal distribution does not actually exist. It is not a fact of nature. Rather, it is a mathematical model, an idealisation that can be used to represent data collected in behavioural research" (Shavelson, 1996, p. 12) The law of probability and the normal curve that illustrates it are based on the law of chance or the probable occurrence of certain events.

1. The curve is symmetrical around its vertical axis – 50% of the scores are above the mean and 50% below the mean.
2. The mean, median, and the mode of the distribution have the same value.
3. The items cluster around the centre – most scores are near the mean, median, and mode with fewer scores far away from the centre.
4. The curve has no boundaries in either direction, for the curve never touches the base line, no matter how far it is extended. The curve is a curve of probability, not of certainty.

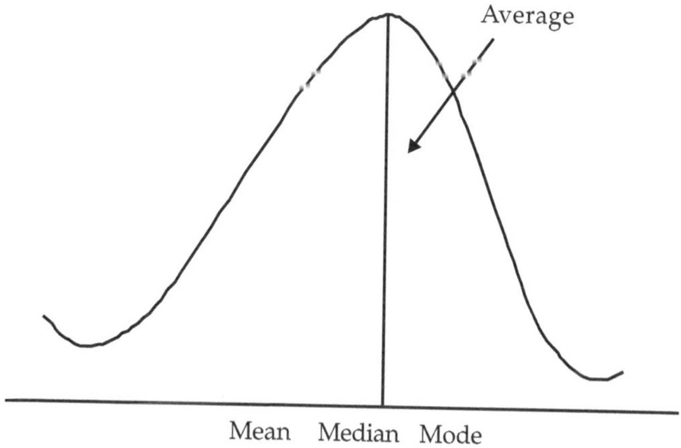


when there is lack of symmetry in a curve, we get skewness and kurtosis.

## 1. Skewness

A distribution is said to be skewed when its mean and median fall at different points in the distribution. Sknewness is of two kinds – positive skewness and negative skewness.

In the negative skewness, the distributions are said to be skewed negatively or to the left when scores are massed at the high end of the scale and are spread out more gradually towards the low end.

**Negative Skewness:**

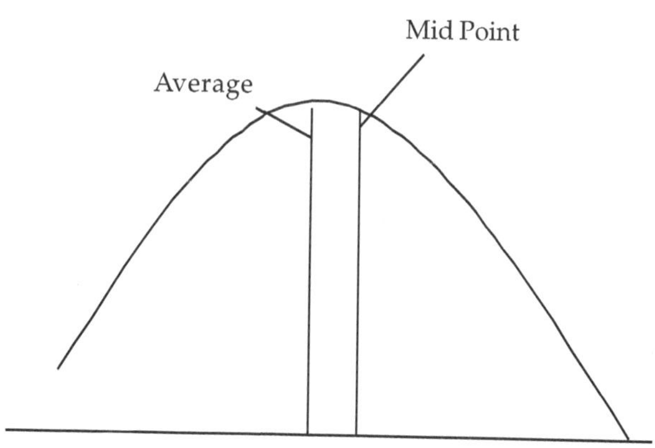

**Positive Skewness:**

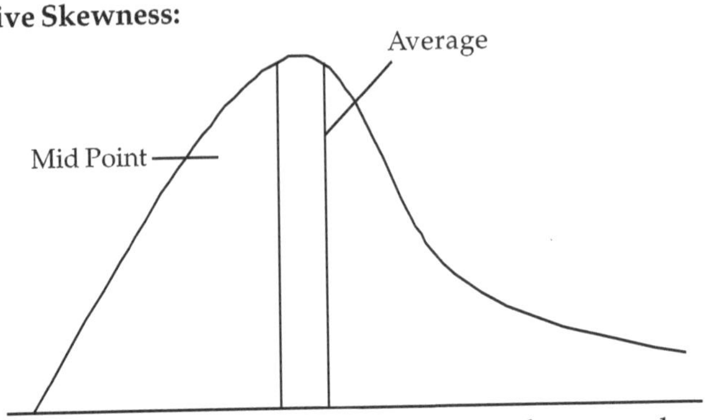


They are said to be skewed positively or to the right when scores are massed at the low end and are spread out gradually towards the high end. The mean is pulled more towards the skewed end of the distribution than is the median. Naturally, the greater the gap between the mean and median, the greater the skewness.

**2. Kurtosis**

The term kurtosis refers to the peakness or flatness of a frequency distribution as compared with the normal.

When a frequency distribution is more peaked than the normal, it is said to be lepto kurtic; one flatter than the normal, is called platy kurtic.

$$\text{Ku} = \frac{Q}{P_{90} + P_{10}} \text{ where}$$

$$\text{Q is equal to } \frac{Q_3 - Q_1}{2}$$

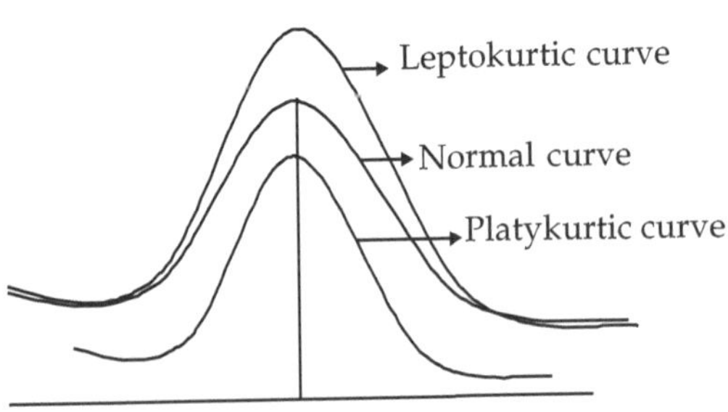

## Measures of Relative Position

Standard scores provide a method of expressing any score in a distribution in terms of its distance from the mean in standard deviation units. The utility of this conversion of a raw score to a standard score will become clear as each type is introduced and illustrated. Three types of standard scores are considered.

1. Z score (Sigma)
2. T score (T)
3. College board score ($Z_{cb}$)

Remember that the distribution is assumed to be normal when using any type of standard score.

### 1. The Z score (Sigma)

In describing a score in a distribution, its deviation from the mean expressed in standard deviation units is often more meaningful than the score itself. The unit of measurement is the standard deviation.

$$z = \frac{X - \bar{X}}{\sigma} \text{ or } \frac{X}{\sigma}$$

where X = raw score

$\bar{X}$ = mean

σ = standard deviation

x = ( X - $\bar{X}$ ) score deviation from the mean

### 2. The T Score (T)

Although the z score is most frequently used, it is sometimes awkward to have negatives or scores with decimals. Therefore, another version of a standard score, the T score, has been devised to avoid some confusion resulting from negative z scores (below the mean) and also to eliminate decimal values.

$$T = 50 + 10\frac{X - \bar{X}}{\sigma} \text{ or } 50 + 10z$$

### 3. College board score ($Z_{cb}$)

The college entrance examination board and several other testing agencies use another conversion that provides a more precise measure by spreading out the scale.

$$Zcb = 500 + 100\frac{X - \bar{X}}{\sigma} = 500 + 100z$$

The mean of this scale is 500

The standard deviation is 100

The range is 200 - 800.

## Measures of Relationship (Correlation)

Correlation is the relationship between two or more paired variables or two or more sets of data. The degree of relationship is measured and represented by the coefficient of correlation. This coefficient may be identified by either the letter r, the Greek letter rho () or other symbols, depending on the data distributions and the way the coefficient has been calculated.

### 1. Linear correlation

This is the simplest kind of correlation to be found between the two sets of scores or variables. Actually, when the relationship between two sets of scores or variables can be represented graphically by a straight line, it is known as Linear Correlation. The correlation between two sets of measures of variables can be positive or negative. It is said to be positive when an increase (or decrease) in one corresponds to an increase (or decrease) in the other. It is negative when increase corresponds to decrease or positive when decrease corresponds to increase. There is also possibility of third type of correlation i.e. zero correlation between the two sets of measures or variables if there exists no relationship between them.

### 2. Coefficient of correlation

For expressing the degree or relationship quantitatively between two sets of measures or variables we usually take the help of an index that is known as coefficient of correlation.

It is a kind of ratio which expresses the extent to which changes in one variable are accompanied by changes in the other variable. It involves no units and varies from – 1 (indicating perfect negative correlation) to + 1 (indicating perfect positive correlation). In case the coefficient of correlation is zero, it indicates zero correlation between two sets of measures.

**Computation of Coefficient of Correlation**

There are two different methods of computing coefficient of correlation

(a) Rank difference method

(b) product moment method

**(a) Rank correlation**

The rank correlation co-efficient is also known as spearman's correlation co-efficient and designated by the symbol ρ' (read as 'rho') The formula for finding the value of P is

$$\rho = 1 - \frac{6\Sigma D^2}{n(n^2 - 1)}$$

Where D is the difference between the ranks, n is the number of pairs of ranks.

Computation of Rank Correlation

Rank correlation can be computed as shown below:

$$\rho = 1 - \frac{6\Sigma D^2}{n(n^2 - 1)} = \rho = 1 - \frac{6\Sigma D^2}{n(n^2 - 1)}$$

| Students | SC score | Math score | Rank in SC | Rank in Maths | d | d2 |
|---|---|---|---|---|---|---|
| A | 90 | 78 | 1 | 2 | -1 | 1 |
| B | 89 | 69 | 2 | 3 | -1 | 1 |
| C | 78 | 87 | 3 | 1 | +2 | 4 |
| D | 48 | 36 | 6 | 5 | +1 | 1 |
| E | 56 | 63 | 5 | 4 | +1 | 1 |
| F | 61 | 30 | 4 | 6 | -2 | 4 |
| | | | | | $\Sigma d = 0$ | $\Sigma d^2 = 12$ |

$$\rho = 1 - \frac{6\times 12}{6(36-1)} = \frac{6\times 12}{6\times 35} = \frac{72}{210}.342 \quad 1-.348 = 0.658$$

ρ = .658 There is positive correlation between the variables

**Product Moment Method of Computing Co-efficient of Correlation**

This method is also known as Pearson Product Moment method in the honour of the English statesman Karl Pearson who is said to be the inventor of this method. The coefficient of correlation computed by this method is known as Product Moment coefficient of correlation and symbolically represented by 'r'.

(a) The calculation of 'r' from ungrouped data. The basic formula for the computation of 'r' for the ungrouped data by this method is:

$$r = \frac{\Sigma xy}{\sqrt{\Sigma x^2, \Sigma y^2}}$$ where x and y represent the deviation

of scores in the tests X and Y from the means of each distribution.

**Graphical Representation of Ungrouped Data**

We use the following common graphs for the data not grouped into a frequency distribution.

For the data not grouped into a frequency distribution we use the following common graphs: *(i)* bar graphs; *(ii)* circle diagram or pie diagram; *(iii)* pictograph; and *(iv)* line graphs.

**Computation of Coefficient of Correlation**

Coefficient of correlation can be computed for grouped data and ungrouped data as shown below.

$$r = \frac{\Sigma dx \Sigma dy}{\sqrt{\Sigma dx^2 \Sigma dy^2}}$$

| X | Y | d – dx / x | Y – dy – y | dx dy | $dx^2$ | $dy^2$ |
|---|---|---|---|---|---|---|
| 8 | 4 | +3 | -2 | 6 | +9 | 4 |
| 2 | 8 | -3 | +2 | -6 | +9 | 4 |
| 5 | 7 | 0 | +1 | 0 | 0 | 1 |
| 3 | 6 | -2 | 0 | 0 | +4 | 0 |
| 7 | 5 | +2 | -1 | -2 | +4 | 1 |
| $\Sigma x = 25$ | $\Sigma y = 30$ | | | -14 | $\Sigma dx^2 = 26$ | $\Sigma dy^2 = 10$ |

$$r = \frac{\Sigma dx \Sigma dy}{\sqrt{\Sigma dx^2 \Sigma dy^2}} = \frac{-14}{\sqrt{26 \times 10}} = \frac{-14}{\sqrt{260}} = \frac{-14}{16.12} = -0.868$$

There is a negative high correlation between the two variables

**Coefficient of Correlation (Grouped Data)**

$$r = \frac{n\Sigma xy - (\Sigma x)(\Sigma y)}{\sqrt{[n\Sigma x^2 - (\Sigma x)^2][n\Sigma y^2 - (\Sigma y)^2]}}$$

| Student | Arithmetic score X | Reading score Y | $x^2$ | $y^2$ | xy |
|---|---|---|---|---|---|
| A | 8 | 7 | 64 | 49 | 56 |
| B | 7 | 4 | 49 | 16 | 28 |
| C | 6 | 5 | 36 | 25 | 30 |
| D | 5 | 8 | 25 | 64 | 40 |
| E | 3 | 3 | 9 | 9 | 9 |
| F | 9 | 8 | 81 | 64 | 72 |
| | $\Sigma x = 38$ | $\Sigma y = 35$ | $\Sigma x^2 = 264$ | $\Sigma y^2 = 227$ | $\Sigma xy = 235$ |

$$r = \frac{n\Sigma xy - (\Sigma x)(\Sigma y)}{\sqrt{[n\Sigma x^2 - (\Sigma x)^2][n\Sigma y^2 - (\Sigma y)^2]}}$$

$$= \frac{6 \times 235 - 38 \times 35}{\sqrt{(6 \times 264 - 1444)(6 \times 227 - 1225)}}$$

$$= \frac{1410-1330}{\sqrt{(1584-1444)*(1362-1225)}} = \frac{80}{\sqrt{140 \times 137}}$$

$$= \frac{80}{\sqrt{19180}} = \frac{80}{138.49} = 0.57$$

The correlation in high positive.

## GRAPHICAL REPRESENTATION OF GROUPED DATA

We can graphically represent the frequency distribution by following the method of: *(i)* The histogram; *(ii)* The frequency polygon; and *(iii)* The cumulative frequency curve (ogive)

### The Histogram

A two dimensional frequency diagram is called a histogram. A histogram is essentially a bar graph of a frequency distribution. It shows what proportions of cases fall into each category.

| Class interval | 50 | 60 | 70 | 80 | 90 | 100 | 110 |
|---|---|---|---|---|---|---|---|
| Frequency | 5 | 8 | 12 | 18 | 10 | 6 | 1 |

**Histogram**

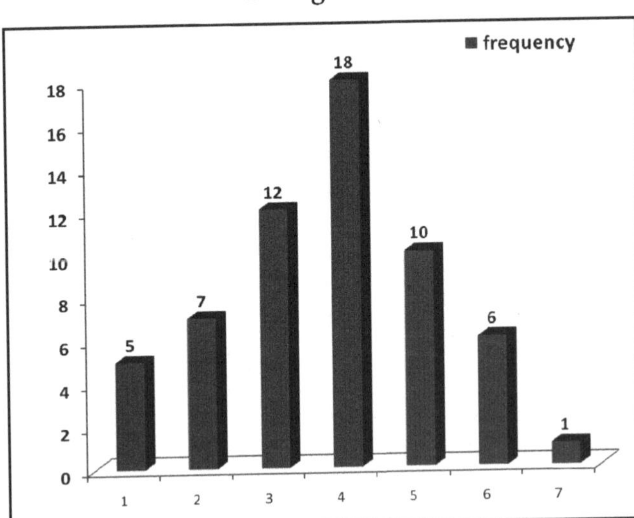

**Frequency Polygon**

A frequency polygon is a graphical display of a frequency table. The intervals are shown on the X-axis and the number of scores in each interval is represented by the height of a point located above the middle of the interval. The points are connected so that together with the X-axis they form a polygon.

Frequency polygons are useful for comparing distributions. This is achieved by overlaying the frequency polygons drawn for different data sets. In a frequency distribution the mid value of each class is obtained. Then on the graph paper, the frequency is plotted against the corresponding mid value. These points are joined by straight lines. These straight lines may be extended in both dimensions to meet the X-axis to form a polygon. One way to form a frequency polygon is to connect the mid points at the top of the bars of a histogram with a smooth curve. Of course, the mid points themselves could easily be plotted without the histogram and be joined by line segments. Sometimes it is beneficial to show the histogram and frequency polygon together. Unlike histograms, frequency polygon can be super imposed so as to compare several frequency distributions.

**Cumulative Frequency Curve (Ogive)**

A cumulative frequency curve (also known as an ogive) is a graphical representation of the number of items that have values that are either above or below a given level. It is also described as the running total of all the given frequencies. In order to illustrate this curve, one must start off by drawing a graph that places the cumulative frequency values along a vertical line, (Y-axis) while placing the intervals on the horizontal line, (X-axis). Then the appropriate points from the data are then potted on this graph and these points are connected by a single line to form the cumulative frequency curve. Cumulative frequency is obtained by adding the frequency of a class interval and the frequencies of the proceeding intervals up to that class interval. We can draw cumulative frequency curve for the following marks obtained by sixty students in English achievement test.

| Class Interval | Actual Class Limits | Mid Point | Frequency | Less than Cumulative Frequency | More than Cumulative Frequency |
|---|---|---|---|---|---|
| 40 - 50 | 39.5 - 49.5 | 45 | 5 | 5 | 60 |
| 50 - 60 | 49.5 - 59.5 | 55 | 8 | 13 | 55 |
| 60 - 70 | 59.5 - 69.5 | 65 | 12 | 25 | 42 |
| 70 - 80 | 69.5 - 79.5 | 75 | 18 | 43 | 35 |
| 80 - 90 | 79.5 - 89.5 | 85 | 10 | 53 | 17 |
| 90 - 100 | 89.5 - 99.5 | 95 | 6 | 59 | 7 |
| 100 - 110 | 99.5 - 109.5 | 105 | 7 | 60 | 1 |

Cumulative Frequency curve (ogive)

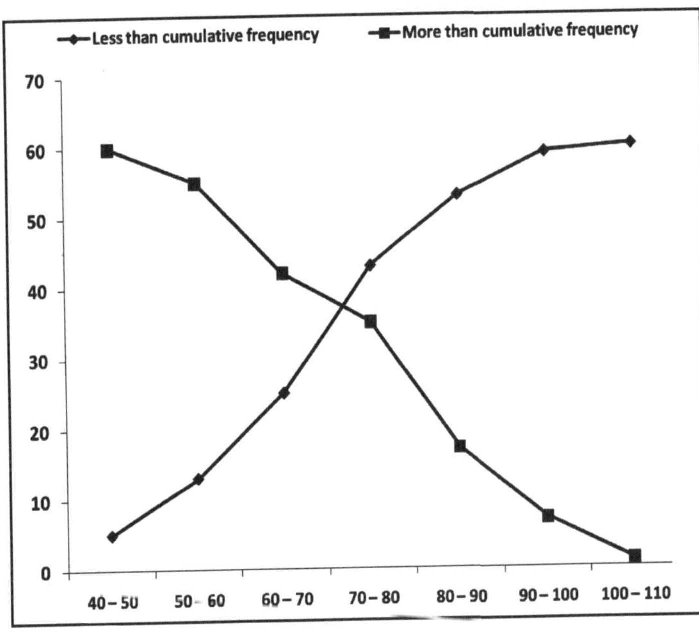


For the given data we have to calculate less than cumulative frequency and more than cumulative frequency as shown in the table. Now we have drawn two curves viz less than cumulative frequency curve and more than cumulative frequency curve. These two curves cut at Mid-point. If we draw a horizontal and vertical line from the mid-point. We get mean for e.g., The vertical line from the Mid point shows 72 in the X axis

Mean is = 72 and the horizontal line shows 40 in the Y axis. It is cf = 40, hence cumulative frequency is = 40. Mean is = 72.

## SUMMARY

Statistics is a body of mathematical techniques or processes for gathering, organising, analysing and interpreting numerical data. Statistics is a basic tool of measurement, evaluation and research. There are two types of recognised data in the application of statistical treatments. They are parametric data and non parametric data.

There are two types of satistical analysis. They are descriptive analysis and inferential analysis. Descriptive analysis limits generalistation to the particular group of individuals. No conclusions are extended beyond that group. Inferential analysis draws conclusions about population based on samples.

Several basic types of statistical measures are appropriate in describing and analysing data in a meaningful way. They are measures of central tendency or averages, measures of spread or dispersion, measures of relative position and measures of relationship.

Non statisticians use averages to describe the characteristics of groups in a general way. But to the statisticians the term average is unsatisfactory. The most useful averages in educational research are the mean, the median and the mode. The mean is arithmetic average. The median is a point above and below which one half of the scores fall. The mode is the most occurring score.

Measures of variability or disperson are used for the comparison of two or more sets of scores. There are four measures of spread or dispersion. They are range, the quartile deviation, the average deviation, and standard deviation. Range is the difference between the highest and the lowest scores. Quartile deviation is the semi interquartile range. Average deviation is the mean of the deviations of all the separate scores in the series. Standard deviation is the square root of variance.

Normal probability curve is a mathematical model, an idealisation used to represent data collected in behavioural research. A distribution is said to be skewed when its mean and median fall at different position. Skewness is of two kinds: positive skewness and negative skewness. Kurtosis refers to the peakness or flatness of a frequency distribution. Leptokurtic refers to peaked distribution and platykurtic refers to flatter distribution.

Measures of relative position include Z score, T score and college board score. The Z score refers to the deviation from the mean expressed in standard deviation. T score is another version of a standard score devised to avoid confusion resulting from negative Z scores and to eliminate decimal values. College board score is another conversion that provides a more precise measure by spreading out the scale.

Correlation is the relationship between two or more paired variables or two or more sets of data. When the relationship between two sets of scores or variables can be represented graphically by a straight line, it is known as linear correlation. Coefficient of correlation is a kind of ratio which expresses the extent to which changes in one variable are accompanied by changes in the other variable.

For graphical representation of ungrouped data we use bar diagrams, pie diagram, pictograph and line graph. For graphical representation of grouped data we use histogram, frequency polygon and the cumulative frequency curve (Ogive).

# 9

# Listening Comprehension

## LISTENING

Listening is paying attention to somebody or something. (eg) oral presentation or musical sounds. Listening is paying attention to sound and sense. Listening is the skill children acquire first. Listening takes place from womb to tomb. Listening is the foremost skill. It leads to development of other skills. Listening is more than merely hearing words. Listening is an active process by which students receive, construct meaning from and respond to spoken and or nonverbal messages. (Emmert, 1994). It forms an integral part of the communication process and should not be separated from the other language arts. Listening comprehension complements reading comprehension. Verbally clarifying the spoken message before, during and after a presentation enhances listening comprehension.

## KINDS OF LISTENING

Wolvin and Coakely (1992) have identified four different kinds of listening. They are:

- *Comprehensive (Informational) Listening* – students listen for the content of the message.
- *Critical (Evaluative) Listening* – Students judge the message.
- *Appreciative (Aesthetic) Listening* – Students listen for enjoyment.
- *Therapeutic (Empathetic) Listening* – Students listen to support others but not judge them.

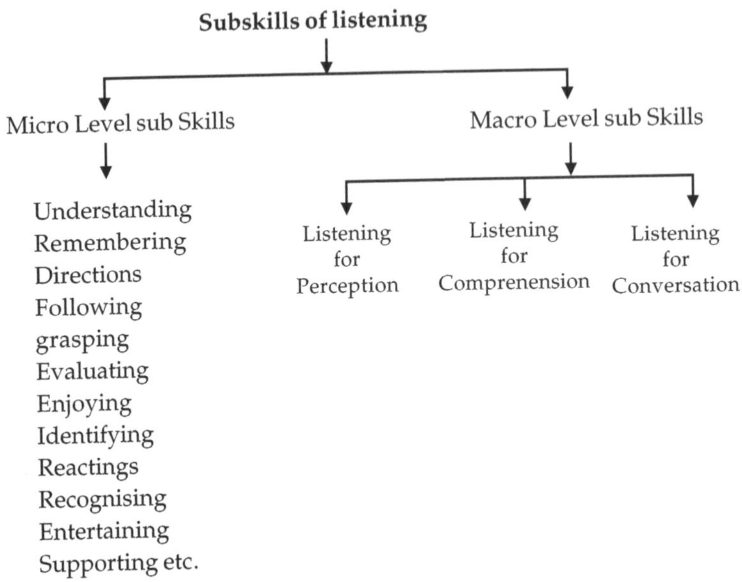


## STAGES OF LISTENING

Listening process includes seven stages as shown below:

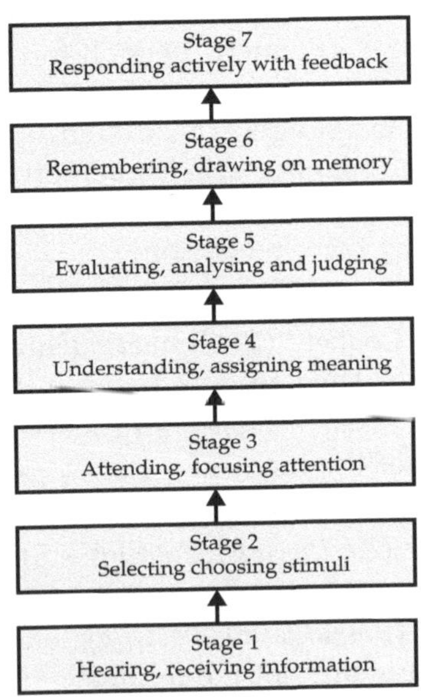

## MACRO SUB SKILLS OF LISTENING

There are two important subskills of listening. They are: *(i)* Listening for perception; and *(ii)* Listening for comprehension.

### Listening for Perception

Perception means the way we notice and understand the true nature of thing. In listening for perception, the learner is given practice in identifying the different sounds combination, stress and intonation pattern of spoken English.

Listening for perception is practised more at primary and middle school levels.

Here the focus is on aural perception.

The listening exercises do not use visuals.

Students are required to concentrate on sounds.

Teacher pronounces and the students imitate.

Students are drilled how to differentiate sounds. The students should underline the correct word used by the teacher

Pin Bin Pun Bun

Pit Bit Sun Shun

I want the house painted in light green

I want the house painted in light cream

Bring the glass here. Bring the class here

### Listening for Comprehension

Comprehension refers to the ability to understand fully. Listening for comprehension is more relevant at middle and secondary levels. Listening material is based on particular context. Learner is given practice in specific areas related to his/her needs. Thus listening leads to speaking. Listening activities have an element of game playing and problem solving built into them.

## THREE PHASES OF LISTENING

There are three phases of listening. They are: *(i)* The pre-listening phase; *(ii)* The while listening phase; *(iii)* The post listening phase.

### The pre-listening Phase

This phase includes asking for question and introduction. Listening will enable the pupils to ask for directions, to follow direction and to give directions clearly. In this phase the teacher sets up activities. It helps the learner to understand the context and to respond. The pre listening activities are very short.

**The While – Listening Phase**

During this phase, the learner completes the task based on the listening materials. It helps them to concentrate on the listening activity rather than worry about grammar or reading. Learners gather as much information as possible. The focus is on the message of the listening text. The while listening tasks can be graded carefully.

**The Post – Listening Phase**

In this phase, answers to the listening tasks are discussed. If many students get an item wrong, the relevant portion on the tape can be played back once more and the cause for confusion can be discussed. Speaking skills can be integrated with listening. Similarly, writing skill may be integrated by asking learners to write their responses.

**Listening Materials**

There are three kinds of listening materials, that we can use to teach listening, They are.

1. Authentic listening materials
2. Recorded listening materials
3. Live listening materials

**Using Authentic Materials**

Authentic materials are the speeches in real life situations. It provides learners with the real life listening tasks. They hear real speech. Here, the language may be difficult to understand. It may be fast, rambling and repetitive. It cannot be graded. So it may be unsuitable to the learners level. This can be overcome by giving the learners notes and pre – listening tasks. Real life dialogues and discussions can also be used:

**Using Recorded Listening Materials**

Recorded materials are listening inputs. They are specially designed for teaching purpose. Developed listening materials have accompanying audio cassettes and worksheets.

### Live Listening Materials

Live materials include listening to TV, radio, news, weather report, sports commentary, panel discussion etc. This provides intensive aural practice to learners. It includes listening information, listening to specific for general understanding to reduce meaning, to form opinion and attitude etc.

### Listening Activities

There are some listening comprehension activities. Learner is required to listen and make a response. There is listening to text and reading at the same time. Listening to text does not develop learners' skill of listening comprehension. There are certain specific activities to promote listening and comprehension skill. They are: *(i)* dictation; *(ii)* listening and following a route; *(iii)* listening to a telephone call; *(iv)* listening to commentaries; *(v)* listening to instruction; and *(vi)* jigsaw listening.

### Dictation

Dictation is the art of speaking or reading so that somebody can write down the words. It is the most common listening exercise. It makes the learner actively involved in language learning. Teacher plans the activity properly to make it meaningful and interesting. Teacher dictates words and students write the words. They pool all the words. They write a story using the words. Pair work can be used effectively. Student A may dictate and student B may write. Then B may dictate and A may write. So the students are not only listening but also writing.

### Listening and Following Route

In this activity a route map is used. Exercises are designed to link the spoken description with the map. The teacher wants the students to make the route. The teacher gives necessary instructions and comments. In this way, a real life context is introduced. The listening becomes more interesting.

### Listening to a Telephone Call

Middle school learners are required to make phone calls for formal and informal, purposes. Listening is the key element in telephone skills. The listener should write down the important details. Teachers should use the important details. Teachers should use the word known to the students. The telephone communication should take into account the age and experience level of the students.

**Listening to Commentaries**

Listening to commentaries is a good listening activity. The students listen to commentaries for specific information. The student uses the background sound for clues. The same listening material can be used for other classes also by designing a new worksheet.

**Listening to Instruction**

In this activity, the students listen to the instruction of the teacher and mark it in the map or diagrams, ground plan or flow charts. They can use school festival for practice. Students may mark the stalls as they listen to the teachers. At higher class, students can be called out in random. Real life context is used here. So the activity is interesting for the students.

**Jigsaw Listening**

Jigsaw listening is a kind of listening activity. Teacher divides the class into groups. Each group listens to a part of a story on audio cassette. In the next stage, each group sends one or two students to other groups to collect the missing information. The various groups thus collect all missing information. Finally, they speculate on the last or the ending part of the story. Mystery story is ideal for this type of activity. It requires multiple recordings. Many tape recorders will be needed to save time and to avoid waiting of other groups. Finally, the teacher plays the last part of the story.

## SUMMARY

Listening is paying attention to somebody or something. Listening is paying attention to sound and sense. Listening process includes seven stages such as hearing or receiving information, selecting stimuli, focusing attention, understanding meaning evaluating, remembering and responding actively with feedback.

There are four kinds of listening. They are comprehensive listening, critical listening, appreciative listening and therapeutic listening. Listening includes micro level sub skills and macro level subskills. Macro level subskills are listening for perception, listening for comprehension and listening for appreciation conversation.

Micro level subskills include many skills. The important micro level sub skills are understanding, remembering, following directions, evaluating grasping, enjoying, identifying, reacting, recognising, entertaining and supporting. Development of adequate micro level sub skills will tell upon the listening as well as the speaking skills of the students.

There are three phases of listening. They are the pre-listening phase, the while listening phase and the post listening phase. The three kinds of listening materials widely used to develop listening skills in students are authentic listening materials, recorded listening materials and live listening materials.

There are some listening comprehension activities learner is required to listen to and make a response. The specific activities that can be used to promote listening and comprehension skills in students are dictation, listening and following route, listening to a telephone call, listening to commentaries, listening to instruction and jigsaw listening.

# 10 Speaking Skill

## SPEAKING

Speaking is conveying ideas, emotions, feelings etc through words to other. Speaking is the most demanding skill for the teacher. Developing speaking skill in students is an arduous task. Children are able to express their thoughts in mother tongue. Such skill they should develop in using English language also. Students do not have adequate opportunity to practise speaking English outside the classroom. So they should be adequately trained in the classroom itself.

## TWO MAJOR COMPONENTS OF SPEAKING SKILLS

Speaking skill has two major components. They are:

1. Motor perceptive skills
2. Interaction skills

### Motor Perceptive Skills

Motor perceptive skills are the skills in perceiving, recalling and articulating the sounds and structures of the languages in correct order. These skills are to be developed at primary level by means of look and say exercise or pattern practice. Usually there is no context. Learners have to develop these skills through repetition and chorus drill. Martin Bygate (1987) criticises this stage. This is like learning to drive without ever going out on the road. Learners face problem in transferring their knowledge from a language learning situation to language using situation. (Wilkins)

### Interaction Skills

Interaction skill refers to the ability to converse with others. Interaction skills involve knowing what to say, how to say and how to establish and maintain contact with other persons. Interaction skills enable the learner to transfer his or her knowledge, from a language learning situation. Now there is a growing emphasis on teaching and learning conversation/oral skills. Controlled exercises, used in the language class by giving practice in structures have now given way to dynamic and meaningful oral practice.

## TECHNIQUES OFTEACHING ORAL SKILLS

The following are the major techniques of teaching oral skills. They are: *(i)* conversation class; *(ii)* topic based discussion class; *(iii)* task centred fluency practice.

### Conversation Class

Conversation class is very effective to develop oral skills. Teacher sits with students. He interacts with them by asking simple questions about their home, family, village etc. It is usually a question answer session. It is not productive or creative. Conversation class lacks interesting and clearly defined topics.

### Topic Based Discussion Class

Topic based discussion class is a fluency based activity. Teacher plans discussion on interesting topics. This is better than conversation class because here discussion is structured and clear. But the learners don't show interest in speaking. This highlights a crucial fact of learning. Learners need a reason to speak, not a topic to speak about. Another disadvantage is that this is carried out in the whole class. So the discussion is often dominated by the bright students.

### Task Centred Fluency Practice

Now importance is given to communicative language teaching. So task centred fluency practice is used more and more. In this, a group is given a task to perform through verbal interaction. It may be a group activity or a role play. Performing the task results in giving a group report, a speech or presentation. This practice enhances the fluency of the students. It also provides a basis for feedback.

## TASKS FOR DEVELOPING SPEAKING SKILLS

The exercises under language function and speech are very useful to improve speaking skill. Pictures and objects can also be used to develop speaking skills. Teacher asks question based on pictures or objects, Students answer the questions. Speaking skill can be developed through text book exercises. The following are the tasks to develop speaking skills: *(i)* individual work; *(ii)* pair work; *(iii)* group work.

### Individual Work

Pupils can be trained in monologue, role-play activities such as speech, talk, a lecture, seminar presentation, a debate etc. Teacher should provide help and guidelines whenever necessary.

### Pair Work

A pair refers to two students. The class is divided into a number of pair groups like A-B, C-D and so on. Flash cards of some words in duplicate are prepared. One set of flash card is given to one group and the other set of flash card to the other group. One students stands up and shows a flash card to other group. The student of the other group reads aloud and vice versa. Thus, there is a healthy competition between the two groups. This task develops speaking skills.

### Group Work

Group work is very effective in developing oral skills. According to research evidence a student does not get even one minute for speaking activity in normal classroom. Group work ensures maximum participation of students. Groupwork gives adequate opportunity for students to speak in small groups. It reduces hesitation and inhibition. It gives a sense of closeness and belongingness to the group. It establishes an effective personal relation. Students can interact with his group members and with other groups. Group work provides opportunity for peer teaching. Students are more likely to learn from each other than from the teacher.

## IMPROVING ORAL FLUENCY

Fluency is the ability to speak independently with ease and spontaneity. The aim of oral drill is to help pupils to acquire fluency. Drills provide learners with many opportunities to hear, to see and to say. Action pictures and speech can be used to provide fluency drill to the students. The following techniques can be used to improve oral fluency.

Parallel sentences

Conversation (Telephoning), interview

Dialogue

Role play

Dramatisation, play enacting, group discussion

Story-telling

**Parallel Sentences**

Teacher gives a sentence for a particular pattern. The pupils are asked to change either the subject or the verb or the object and generate parallel sentences of their own.

E.g.: SVO Pattern—— | He plays football
He plays volley ball (object changed)
He likes football (verb changed)
They like football (subject changed)

**Conversation**

Conversation refers to talk between two or more people. In the conversation class, class is divided into two groups. For each group conversation cards with questions and answers are given. Each student should ask the question from his card. The pupil from the other group should answer. Social interaction among family members, classmates and peers also develops conversation skill of students. Informal conversation is a skill used throughout life. It is the basis for formal speech. Some teachers have conversation corner or place. Students go in pair or small groups for the purpose of chatting together. It develops oral fluency of the students.

**Telephoning**

Telephone conversation develops the oral fluency of the students. Students should know how to use telephone in emergency situation. Role playing can boost telephone practice.

**Interview**

Interviews are more formal conversations. Mock interviews can develop conversation skill of students.

**Dialogue**

Dialogue is a conversation in a book, play or film. Spoken English blossoms only in dialogues. Dialogue establishes a firm link between language and situation. They accommodate the key structures of the language. The dialogue should be relevant to the situation. It should be interesting, it should not be too long. It should express a concept. It is the best suited way to develop fluency. Dialogues are the carriers of culture and tradition. It is effective in developing oral fluency.

**Role Play**

Role play is acting out a role assigned or assumed or undertaken. In real life we play different roles. A man plays the role of a father, role of a husband, role of son to his mother, role of a brother, role of a processional, role of a friend etc. Role play is different from playing a role. Playing a role is actual. But role playing is imaginary.

**Dramatisation**

Dramatisation refers to enacting a scene or play. It is suitable for children because they like to imitate and mimicry. It gives confidence to shy and withdrawn pupils. It helps them to speak aloud and improve their speaking abilities. There are two kinds of dramatisation namely. (i) *Fixed* in which words are memorised; (ii) *Free* in which actors speak in own words.

Teacher tells the story and the students dramatise. This ultimately develops their speaking abilities.

**Play Reading**

Small playlets can be used to improve pupil's English knowledge. It will take only a few minutes to enact these plays. No elaborate arrangement is needed. "Two minutes plays" by Broughton is very effective for this purpose. Students of higher classes can enact long scenes or long plays.

### Group Discussion

Group discussion refers to exchanging and sharing of information among a group of persons. Usually, group discussion sessions are conducted to assess students' intellectual qualities, social traits, mental caliber, personality suitability to a job or course and to judge their awareness about the happening around them.

### Group Size

Number of participants in group discussion must be balanced. If the number of students in a group is large, all may not get adequate opportunity to speak. Discussion may become noisy. Some students may tend to avoid participation in group discussion. Group cannot be small also. If small, there will be lack of diversity of opinion, knowledge and skill. Five to nine members in a group is ideal.

### Nature of Group Discussion

Group discussion is different from meeting. In a meeting, there is a chairperson to conduct the meeting. In group discussion, there is no chairperson. Any member in the group can control the group discussion. In group discussion the formalities are minimum.

### Two Methods of Group Discussion

Usually two methods are followed in group discussion:

1. *Preplanned group discussion:* Here topic is given beforehand. The participants come prepared and discuss
2. *On the spot group discussion:* In this discussion, topic is given at the time of meeting. The participants discuss.

### Story Telling

Story telling is narrating story to others. It is a great tool in teaching. There is no definite way of telling a story. Story telling is an individual art. Each one has his/her own technique. Stories relevant to the concept/lesson should be narrated. Teacher must use familiar stories.

### Preparing for Story Telling

First try to get the story live. Once the story is clear, focus on how to present it. Tell the story to others to prepare for your story session. Give special attention to the beginning. Don't give away the plot. Convey the feeling and emotions of the character.

**Story Telling Skills**

- In story telling, one should vary the volume of pitch and tempo of voice.
- Use face, body and gestures
- Make face and body respond to tale. Have a clear focus and maintain concentration.
- Maintain engaging eye contact with the listeners
- Use different exaggerated character voices. Remember to regain your style as narrater. Use silence and pauses to add dramatic effect

**Advantages**

It promotes an interactive teaching learning experience. It improves the attention span of children. It promotes involvement and participation, It facilitates creativity in students and teachers. It kindles creative imagination in children, increases children's willingness to communicate, encourages active participation, increases verbal proficiency and enchances listening skills. Narration and description are very essential for story telling.

**Narration**

Narration means giving an account of something or telling about something. It is important means of communicating knowledge. It makes the subject matter easy and interesting. Narration is an effective device in teaching language, history and natural sciences.

**Significance of Narration**

It is an essential device for teachers to draw the attention and interest of the students towards the subject. By way of narration, facts must be told and necessary information must be conveyed.

**Objectives**

The main objectives of narration are:

1. To arouse interest and enthusiasm;

2. To develop an ability to understand narratives;
3. To develop an ability to respond in speech as reaction to hearing; and
4. To share ideas and experiences with others.

**Characteristics of Narration**

Narration is an art of speech. Narration involves clear and vivid presentation in logical sequence. It enables listeners to reconstruct happening by imagination.

Principles of Narration

Narration has to be motivating and cause interest

Narrator has to use language effectively

The pupils should recreate the events in their minds

Narration should not be used to indoctrinate

Long narration should be avoided

**Application of Narration**

A competent teacher can use narration for a creative activity

Reproduce a story from a given outline

Complete an incomplete story

Buildup a story from given pictures

Expand proverbs titles into episodes

Narrate significant experience in life.

**Description**

Description means giving a picture of something in words. This is a very important language work. We describe about places, events etc. Description develops our fluency. Description should be clear and detailed. Don't give irrelevant details.

## COMMUNICATION GAMES

These are the games played by the students under the guidance of the teacher. This will develop oral fluency of the students.

**Advantages**

1. These games help students to reinforce the language already learnt.

2. These games improve the student's fluency in listening, speaking, reading and writing.
3. They provide the much needed entertainment

**Procedure**

Teacher divides the class into 4 or 5 groups. Each game has its own rules to be followed. When a group scores a point, it is recorded on the blackboard. The highest scoring group is the winner.

**Kinds of Communication Games:**

There are two major types of communication games. They are:

1. Listening games
2. Speaking games

**Listening Games**

Teacher says, "They must leave ","They must live" students should say whether the two sentences are same or different. This game enhances listening skills.

**Speaking Games**

Spelling games are very useful. Groups are formed. Teacher says the word 'book'. Then first group should say a word starting with 'k'. Suppose they said kind, the next group should give a word starting with 'd'.

**Busy Bee**

Teacher says a word e.g. 'come'. Groups give words starting with 'c'.

*The ladder:* Teacher gives one word i.e. 'hospital'. Groups give related words i.e. bed, patient, medicine, nurse etc. The group giving more words is the winner.

**Advantages of Games**

- Games are the welcome break from the usual routine
- They are motivating and challenging
- Games provide for various language skills.
- They encourage students to interact and communicate
- They enable students to use the languages.

**Debate**

Debating in English develops speaking skills. Debating is arguing and substantiating with valid evidences. It involves reasoning, argument and counter argument. Speakers can speak for or against the subject of the debate.

**Interview**

Interview is the face to face conversation between the employer and employee. Mock interview in school develops communicative skill of the students. It will reduce tension, shy and inhibition.

**Extempore Speech**

It is a speech made without prior preparation. The topic should be easy and interesting. This is useful to assess students' capacity to speak coherently and in an interesting manner on the given topic.

## BARRIERS TO EFFECTIVE COMMUNICATION

The process of communication is not always smooth. There are many obstacles and hindrances. They are known as barriers of communication.

Barriers refer to the factors that hinder communication. The following are the notable barriers of effective communication.

Code of language
Vocabulary
Culture and background
Pronunciation
Ineffective Communication
Inaccurate translation
Inattention
Loss in transmission
Vague and unclassified assumption
Fear
Noise, distance and time
Impression

**Code of Language**

The speaker and the listener may not share the same language. If the language is not known to the listener, he cannot understand well.

**Vocabulary**

The words used in the conversation should be familiar to the listener. If it is difficult, he cannot understand.

**Culture and Background Knowledge**

If there is cultural difference between the speaker and the listener, the communication will not be effective.

**Pronunciation**

If the pronunciation is bad, the listener cannot understand. The speaker cannot convey his ideas.

**Ineffective Communication**

If the expression is poor, if there is lack of clarity, the communication cannot be effective. Listener cannot understand.

**Inaccurate Translation**

If the translation is inaccurate, it creates confusion. The listener cannot understand.

**Inattention**

If the listener is inattentive, the speaker cannot drive home his points or ideas.

**Loss in Transmission**

In communication much information is lost in the transmission. So the listeners cannot get full ideas.

**Vague and Unclarified Assumption**

If the message is not clear, listeners cannot understand well. Vague presentation will create barriers.

**Fear**

Fear complex affects upward communication. Subordinates cannot communicate properly with superiors.

**Noise, Distance and Timc**

Much noise, long distance and fatigue time affect communication very much. Both speaker and listener will have difficulty in sustaining communication.

**Impression**

To impress others, speakers start speaking in a different way. It causes confusion. It affects communication very much. It is always better to speak in the normal way.

### How to Overcome the Barriers

The following guidelines will help to overcome ineffective communication:

- ❖ Be strong and steady in achieving your goal
- ❖ Develop self interest to develop your skill in communication
- ❖ Know that no one can be a master in a foreign language, everyone is a learner.
- ❖ Enrich your vocabulary through listening and reading
- ❖ Practise regularly and daily practice will make you perfect

Testing Speaking

Testing speaking is difficult. There is constraint of time in testing oral skills Cyril Weir (1983) has proposed a three part frame work to test spoken interaction:

1. Operation-*informational, interactional.*
2. Performance condition-*time available permissible time.*
3. The expected level of performance - *fluency appropriateness, coherence, effectiveness, accuracy and range of vocabulary.*

### SUMMARY

Speaking is conveying ideas, emotions, feelings etc through oral words. Speaking skill has two major components such as motor perceptive skill and interaction skill. The major techniques of teaching oral skills are conversation class, topic based discussion class and task centred fluency practice. Tasks for developing speaking skills include individual work, pair work and group work.

Fluency is the ability to speak independently with ease and spontaneity. The techniques that can be used to improve oral fluency are generating parallel sentences, conducing conversation class, making telephone conversation, conducting mock interviews, dialogue practice, role play, dramatisation, play enacting, group discussion and story telling.

Communication games are the games played by the students under the guidance of the teacher. This develops the oral fluency of the students. There are two major types of communication games. They are listening games and speaking games. Speaking games include spelling games, busy bee game and the ladder games. Debate, interview and extempore speech also can be used to develop communicative skill of the students.

The process of communication is not always smooth. There are many obstacles and hindrances. They are known as barriers of communication. The noteable barriers of effective communication are code of language, vocabulary level, culture and background, pronunciation, ineffective communication, inaccurate translation, inattention, loss in transmission, fear, noise distance and time.

There are certain ways to enable students to overcome ineffective communication. The ways and means include being determined in achieving fluency, developing interest in communication, enriching vocabulary through listening and reading and constant practice. Students should know that no one can be a master in a foreign language, everyone is a learner.

Testing speaking is difficult. There is constraint of time in testing oral skills. Cyril Weir has proposed a three part framework to test spoken interaction. The framework includes: *(i)* operation - informational and interactional; *(ii)* performance condition-time available and permissible time; and *(iii)* the expected level of performance – fluency, appropriateness, coherence, effectiveness, accuracy and range of vocabulary.

# 11

# Reading Skill

## READING

Reading means articulating the language symbols and understanding meaning. For various reasons habit of reading should be developed among our students from the very beginning. According Jasperson reading by students should start after two months of oral work. Scholars like Gurrey believe that there need not be any reading in the first year of teaching English. After the first two or three weeks of oral work and pattern practice, children are ready for reading of words and sentences. Sentence is the unit of speech and of reading. Initially teacher can draw diagrams on the board and write underneath what they are. Pupils read and link the picture and the sentence. Later, sentences may be flashed without picture and the students may read it. Similarly, pictures may be flashed without sentence and students may be asked to recall the sentence. Matching picture and sentence is also a good exercise. A number of games may be played in the classroom to teach reading. E.g. flash cards with commands and students performing it.

## AIMS OFTEACHING READING

1. to learn English accurately
2. to read with correct pronunciation
3. to read with fluency
4. to read with understanding
5. to enable students to find pleasure in reading

6. to enable students to use ideas gained from reading in other situations.
7. to enable pupils to form a habit of reading
8. To enable students to read material in English after school life
9. to widen the eye span. Eye span refers to the number of words our eyes can see in one complete movement.

## PROCESS INVOLVED IN READING

According to West reading is a process of sight, sound and sense. The eyes look at the print, the mouth produces the sound and the mind interprets the meaning.

Effective reading is relating particular symbol or shape to particular sound and specific meaning. Sight is seeing the letters in a word. Sound is producing the letter sounds i.e. pronunciation. Sense is the meaning of the word.

## TYPES OF READING

The main types of reading are: *(i)* reading aloud; *(ii)* silent reading; *(iii)* skimming; *(iv)* scanning; *(vi)* intensive reading; *(vii)* extensive reading.

### Reading Aloud

It is also known as loud reading or oral reading. This is introduced after two months of oral work. Loud reading is a skill to be developed in the early stages. It trains the pupils to link the spoken word with the symbol. It helps them to develop speech with correct pronunciation, stress and intonation.

### Objectives of Loud Reading

The objectives of loud reading are:

- To enable students to read with correct pronunciation, articulation, intonation, stress and rhythm.
- To enable students to read with expression.
- To test students' knowledge of speaking words, phrases and sentences.
- To give practice to the students.
- To enable the students to understand the meaning.
- To prepare pupils for effective silent reading.

**Process**

*Step 1:* A model reading is given by the teacher with correct pronunciation, stress and intonation. Teacher should read clearly and distinctly and quite loudly. This model reading trains the auditory nerves of the students.

*Step 2:* Students read aloud. Teacher corrects the mistakes if any in pronunciation, intonation etc. Corrections should be done after the student finishes his reading. Speed and accuracy must be emphasised:

- The teacher explains word and context
- Teacher points out the possible associations
- Teacher draws the attention of the students to the comparisons and contrast.

**Precautions**

- The loud reading should be done only after the teacher has given a model reading.
- The passage for reading should be within the comprehension level of the students.
- A.W. Freshly suggests, "over-emphasis on reading aloud in the early stages will often promote word by word reading and pattern reading by the teacher may not help in any long term way. Positive measures to improve phrases and recognition may be taken by the institutional material followed by a few questions to make sure that what has been read has also been understood".
- Mistakes in reading should be checked and corrected by the teacher.
- In the beginning speed should not be emphasised.
- The teacher should check students' postures while they read.
- Special attention should be given to weak students.
- Before loud reading, pronunciation drill is essential.

**Advantages**

- Students learn the proper method of reading
- Students develop the skill of speech and giving lectures.
- The mistakes related to pronunciation can be corrected.

- It trains various sensory organs such as eyes, ears and mouth etc.
- Students learn by imitation which is a natural method of learning.

**Limitation**

- In the opinion of E.W. Menzel loud reading is not a source of pleasure.
- It does not help in penetrating the meaning. In this context, A.W. Freshly says. "The danger of too much reading aloud is that it may lead to the short-circuiting of the meaning, whereby the written word does not convey meaning but becomes merely a symbol for the collection of sounds and is translated straight in sound".
- In later life, it is silent reading which is preferred.
- If a student becomes habitual to loud reading, he cannot become an extensive reader.
- Generally the students of a class pay no heed to what the other student is reading aloud.
- Just a few students are benefitted.
- In most of the public places such as library and reading rooms, only silent reading is allowed.

Hence many scholars like Gurrey do not recommend loud reading.

**Silent Reading**

It is reading without making sound. It is the most important reading. After the initial stage, silent reading should be emphasised. It is library reading. In silent reading students are asked to read a passage. They are abstained from making sound, whispering, murmuring or moving lips while reading. Pupils do not stop at punctuation marks. The movement of their eyes stops only at difficult places.

**The Objectives of Silent Reading**

The following are the primary objectives of silent reading:

- To enable the students to read without making sounds and moving lips, so that they may not disturb others.
- To enable students to read with ease, speed and fluency.

- To enable students to read with comprehension.
- To get students' vocabulary expanded.
- To provide for pleasure and profit, to enable the students to read for interest and to get information".

**Process**

*Step 1:* Teacher explains to students about silent reading and its aims

*Step 2:* He asks the students to read a passage silently

*Step 3:* Teacher checks whether the students are whispering or murmuring. He supervises the posture of students.

*Step 4:* After allowing sufficient time, teacher asks questions to test the understanding of students.

**Precautions**

The following precautions should be taken to make silent reading effective:

- Only those passages should be read which can be understood and appreciated by the students.
- Special attention should be paid to weak students.
- The paragraph for reading should not be too long.
- The teacher should be particular about giving students a task of wide reading by gradually selecting fresh and unseen paragraphs.
- Teacher must give necessary instructions before silent reading.
- Teacher must ask comprehension questions after silent reading.
- The duration of silent reading should differ according to the nature of the matter and the standard of the class.

**Advantages of Silent Reading**

The advantages of silent reading are:

- It is time saving and faster and saves the energy.
- It develops the ability to read with interest
- It acts as a deterrant against the tendency so common amongst beginners to translate what they read in English into their mother tongue.

- It is quite useful in later life as it is used in public places and libraries.
- It initiates self-education and deep study.
- It enables attention and energy to be concentrated on meaning and so saves a division of attention resulting in a greater assimilation of information.

**Limitations of Silent Reading**

The limitations of silent reading include:

1. Silent reading is not advantageous for beginners.
2. It does not teach correct pronunciation.
3. It cannot be checked if students are actually reading
4. The mistakes of the students cannot be corrected.
5. It is uninteresting.
6. Sometimes students cannot understand some parts of a passage, but they can not take the help of teachers. According to Morrison, "Reading as an end in foreign language may be confined to silent reading".

**Difference between silent reading and loud reading**

| Loud Reading | Silent Reading |
|---|---|
| Reading by producing sound | Reading without sound |
| Audible to others | Not audible to others |
| Helps to learn pronunciation | Facilitates comprehension |
| Makes one tired | No one feels tired |
| One cannot read much | One can read a lot |
| Loud reading disturbs other | Does not disturb others |
| Childish way of reading | Adult way of reading |
| Suitable for lower classes | Suitable at higher level |

**Skimming**

Skimming is quickly glancing and getting the general idea of the passage. We pick up a book, look at its title page, flip through the pages, have a glance and try to get the general ideas or the content of the book.

**Scanning**

Scanning refers to reading for specific information. We scan book or text to find out a particular piece of specific information. This is just like looking for the departure of a particular train without reading the entire timetable.

## INTENSIVE READING

Intensive reading is a detailed reading. When we read text book or research reports, we do not read for pleasure. We read to understand every detail. Intensive reading involves extracting specific information. In intensive reading, we give importance to new words, grammar, language expression, ideas etc.

## EXTENSIVE READING

Extensive reading refers to reading longer texts like novel, stories etc. This is done for pleasure. This is the main difference between intensive reading and extensive reading. Skipping and skimming is allowed in extensive reading. The main interest lies in getting global idea.

### Procedure

In extensive reading, students read for pleasure. The primary object is general information, not language study. Students should read rapidly. They should locate the topic sentence. They can skip and skim. They ignore certain paragraphs or passages. They concentrate on their interested ones. They should guess the meaning of new words from the context.

### Merits and Importance of Extensive Reading

Extensive reading is important because it enables one to read silently and quickly.

- It helps in assimilation of ideas.
- It keeps the whole class busy and active.
- It increases vocabulary
- It has high 'transfer of learning' value since it prepares the students for library reading.
- It paves the path for individual method of study and self education.

## METHODS OF TEACHING READING

The following are the most important methods of teaching reading: *(i)* alphabet method; *(ii)* phonic method;

*(iii)* phonetic method *(iv)* word method; *(v)* phrase method; *(vi)* sentence method.

**The Alphabetic Method**

It is an old method of teaching reading. In this method, the students are taught the alphabets i.e. A, B, C of English. There the unit of teaching is letter. Later the students learn word by combining alphabets. It is a dull and boring method. It is not good because it is lengthy, tedious and meaningless. There is much emphasis on learning by rote.

**The Phonic Method**

It is a method of teaching reading through basic speech sounds. Word is broken into basic sounds. It facilitates reading. Students learn different sounds first. It is the method used in UK. They learn alphabets later. This method is very effective as forms of letters correspond with their sounds. The only difficulty is that there is need for expert teachers to apply this method.

**The Phonetic Method**

Here 44 sounds of 26 English letters are taught. Teacher explains how different organs of speech produce sounds. He explains how to produce sounds. Here practising correct sound is emphasised. Different consonant sounds are taught. Teacher teaches first same sounds and then contrasting sounds.

**Material Aid**

This method makes use of material aids to teach reading and pronunciation.

*Pronunciation:* *(i)* Charts of speech organs; *(ii)* Position of speech organs while producing different sounds; *(iii)* linguaphone and gramaphone for demonstration of sounds. Now-a-days there are CDs available for this purpose.

**The Word Method**

Wren calls it the one and only rational method to teach reading. Here unit of teaching is word. Pictures with words are used. It is also called look and say method. Students see the pictures and say what they are. It is a popular method. It motivates the learners. This method is better than any other method. Only drawback is that we cannot have pictures for some words i.e. the, to, for, from etc.

**The Phrase Method**

Here the unit of teaching is a phrase. Students learn phrase first and then alphabets. Readers always recognise group of words at each fixation of eyes. So phrase method is emphasised. But this method is not suitable for weak students. They cannot learn two or three words at a time.

**The Sentence Method**

Here sentence is the unit of teaching. Sentence is the unit of speech. So it is a logical method. Words attain meaning with other words before and after them. In this method, the students learn sentence first and then words and alphabets. It helps pupils to understand full meaning. It prevents word by word reading. It lays foundation for all skills. The drawback is that it overstresses memory in the process of learning.

## STRATEGIES TO DEVELOP READING SKILL

Like other language skills, reading is also a complex skill involving a number of simultaneous operations. The teachers can develop in the students the necessary skills of faster reading by allowing the students to read independently. The teachers should cultivate in the students the habit of extensive reading. The materials used for extensive reading should carefully be selected and provided to students. The teacher should also make his students realise the objectives in reading. He should make his students know the literary, linguistic, intellectual, recreational and aesthetic objectives in reading.

The teacher can provide a number of exercises to the students to develop reading comprehension. The teacher should:

- Allow them to read a passage at normal speed.
- Make them understand the lexical and the structural meanings of the words, phrases and sentences.
- Help them to identify incomplete phrases or groups of words at once and when reading aloud allow them to use appropriate sounds, juncture, stress and intonation patterns.

- Help them to guess the meaning of an unfamiliar word from the content.
- Suggest them to consult a dictionary to findout the meaning of the unfamiliar word.
- Teach them to skip over unnecessary passages while skimming for information.
- Advise them to read silently without moving the lips.
- Teach them to distinguish between the writer's opinion and statement of facts.
- Help them to locate the topic sentence of a paragraph.
- Allow them to make a summary of the important points of the passage.
- Teach them to infer the mood of the writer, e.g., serious, jocular, sarcastic etc.
- Teach them to recognise the meaning of various signs, e.g., punctuation marks, paragraphs identification, capitalisation etc.

## TESTING READING

This can be an individual test or group test.

### Individual Test

Teacher has lists of word, phrases and sentences. Each student goes and the teacher asks him to read certain words, phrases and sentences. As the student reads, the teacher assesses his reading skill.

### Group Test

Teacher gives a paragraph with some questions at the end. Students read the passage and answer the questions. Teacher then evaluates their reading skill and comprehension skill. Questions of reading comprehension should suit the age and experience level of the students.

### Types of Comprehension Questions

1. *Plain sense questions* – It requires direct answer – answer can be easily taken from the passage.
2. *Inferential sense questions* – answers cannot be lifted, students should think and answer.
3. *Critical sense questions* – critical analysis and appreciation are required to answer these questions.

**Test for reading**

The following are some of the tests for reading:

**Sentence Making**

Put the following words in your own sentences (single or connected) to make their meaning clear.

Plump

Shrewd

Pile (n)

Cluster (v)

Attempt(v)

Finding out equivalent words:

'Plump rat'

Findout the exact equivalent words in your (pupil's) mother tongue.

## SUMMARY

Reading means articulating the language symbols and understanding meaning. Reading is a process of sight, sound and sense. Sight refers to scanning the letters in a word. Sound refers to producing the letter sounds. Sense refers of understanding the meaning of the word. Sentence is the unit of speech and reading.

There are various types of reading. The main types of reading are reading aloud, silent reading, skimming and scanning, intensive reading and extensive reading. Each type has its own process, advantages and limitations. There are marked differences between loud reading and silent reading, between skimming and scanning and between intensive reading and extensive reading.

There are various methods of teaching reading. Some educators classify the methods of teaching as letter methods and non letter methods. The most important methods of teaching reading include the alphabet method, the phonic method, the phonetic method, word method, phrase method and sentence method.

Like other language skills, reading is also a complex skill involving a number of simultaneous operations. Reading skill of the students can be developed by allowing them to read independently. The habit of extensive reading should be cultivated in students. Teacher should provide a number of exercises to the students to develop their reading comprehension.

There are tests to assess the reading skill of the students. This can be an individual test or a group test. In individual test, reading skill of the students is assessed one by one. In group test, students read the passage and answer the questions and the teacher evaluates their reading skill and comprehension skill.

There are three types of comprehension questions to assess the comprehension skill of the students. They are: *(i)* plain sense questions which require direct answer; *(ii)* inferential sense question for which answers cannot be lifted and students should think and write; and *(iii)* critical sense questions which require critical analysis and appreciation on the part of the students to answer these questions.

# 12 Writing Skill

## WRITING

Writing is expressing ideas, thoughts etc in words. Writing reinforces oral and reading works. It provides a change of activity. It helps to reduce monotony. According to Bacon, *"Reading makes a full man, writing an exact man."*

## MECHANICS OF WRITING

Mechanics refers to how a composition is arranged on paper. Spacing of words, paragraph alignment, spelling, punctuation etc are all parts of mechanics. The rules of mechanics are more like conventions. They are the trends followed by many people. They are altered by creative writers to give special meaning to the text.

### The Purpose of Punctuation

The purposes of punctuation include:

- to help the reader understand the text.
- to clarify grammatical structures
- to give emphasis to certain words and phrases
- to give rhythm or reflect the intonation

## SUB SKILLS IN WRITING

Writing is an effective way of communicating with others. It is a complex activity. It involves many sub skills. They are: *(i)* Visual perception; *(ii)* syntax; *(iii)* organisation; *(iv)* grammar; *(v)* content; *(vi)* purpose; and *(vii)* relevance.

## 1. Visual perception

Visual perception is essential for easy understanding. Pictures can provide visual perception. Pictures have always been popular with good teachers "English Andrew Wright (1989)" lists a number of roles for pictures in language learning:

1. Pictures motivate the student. They make him understand what to pay attention to and to take part.
2. Pictures bring the real world into the classroom and provide a context for language learning.
3. Different responses are possible to pictures; they can be described in an objective way, or interpreted, or responded to subjectively.
4. Pictures can stimulate and provide information which could be referred to in conversation, discussion and story telling.
5. Pictures are easy to prepare, and easy to organise. They are interesting and provide scope for meaningful and authentic use of language.

### Syntax

Syntax is nothing but the formation of sentences or phrases in a particular orderly form in a language. There are many ways of doing this. Paragraphs form a part of any continuous piece of writing in essays, reports, letters etc. Hence paragraphs should be well sequenced. It should have definite plan. E.g. Exemplification of an idea, i.e. a time sequenced organisation of events, comparison, contrast etc. If you want to write to describe a series of events or a process, you must follow some sort of order, usually this order is based on time. In a compare and contrast paragraph you write about similarities and differences between two or more people, places things or ideas in an orderly way. When you write a classification paragraph, you group things or ideas into specific order or categories. There should be order of words in statement questions, order of adjectives, order of verbs etc.

The opening paragraph introduces us to the subject matter or topic and the author's attitude to the subject matter. The purpose of the introductory paragraph is to attract the reader's attention and motivate him/her to read on. The introductory paragraph could be a definition, a question, a proverb, an anecdote, an example, a universal truth, etc. The supporting paragraphs support the main theme in various ways. The concluding paragraph attempts to summarise the essay and provide an impressive conclusion.

**Organisation**

Generally, the organisation of essay consists of three types of paragraphs: introductory, supporting and concluding. Organisation includes introduction, supporting paragraphs and concluding paragraph.

**Grammar**

When we finish writing an essay or a paragraph, we should check whether there is any grammar mistake. We should read it again and again. We should make sure each sentence has a subject. Then we should see whether the subjects and verbs agree with each other and check the verb tenses of each sentence. We should check whether, question form, non finite forms, adjective forms, passive forms, structural words like prepositions, articles conjunctions, auxiliary verbs etc are in correct order. At last we should make sure that each sentence makes sense.

**Content**

When you write an essay, the content should be quite interesting. The content should serve general as well as environmental needs. The content should be simple enough for every one to understand. It should be based on the principle of simple to complex. It should also be presented in a logical sequence. Pictures and illustrations should find a place in the content. They should be attractive and clear. It is the most important part of self education.

**Purpose**

Before putting pen to paper, good writer tries to answer two basic questions. Why am I writing this? Who is supposed to read this? In other words, they have a clear sense of the purpose and the audience. We use language for different purposes. A salesman uses language for persuading the potential customer to buy. A lawyer uses language for arguing and helping his client to win the case. A teacher uses language to help his students understand difficult concepts. If we go on and list all these, there is no end to the uses of language. Though it is the same language, which is used for all these purposes, the choice of words and sentence structures varies from purpose to purpose. Each piece of writing has a different purpose. Students need to practise the writing skills for a variety of purposes. The purpose of writing a report is to inform the readers about the things they don't know. Hence, all necessary details should be included and unnecessary and false information should be avoided.

**Relevance**

Writing skills are complex and difficult. It requires relevant information to write in an appropriate manner for a particular purpose and for a particular audience. If there is lack of relevance, the purpose of writing will not be served.

## WRITING SKILLS

Writing skills include various skills. They are: *(i)* mechanical skill; *(ii)* grammatical skill; *(iii)* judgement skill; *(iv)* discourse skill.

**Mechanical Skill**

Mechanical skill includes a three step process to complete a writing task. The three stages of writing are planning stage, drafting stage and evaluating stage.

*Planning Stage:* During this stage students are taught to engage in a series of strategies.

Group brain storming

Using a jot list followed by a compare – contrast jot list.

Using a paragraph planner

Using a relationship planner

*Drafting stage:* Students are taught several strategies to generate their first draft of a writing project such as:

- Pre writing activities
- Labelling draft by numbers

- Tape recording the information to be used in the written product.
- Suspending judgements about mechanical details like spelling
- Focusing on theme development and coherence.

**Evaluating and Revising Stage**

Students learn to apply a variety of tools to improve their written product such as developing and using guide to evaluate the writing. They evaluate the following for necessary revision or refinement i.e. organisation and theme development, style, spelling and conventions. Proof reading is done to make the writing error free. Critical analysis is done through peer editing conferences. They should use references like thesaurus to verify usages. Transition words must be used for clarifying relationships.

**Grammatical Skills**

Under this category, grammatical skills, we include all items of knowledge and abilities necessary for the construction of correct sentences.

1. ability to understand and use grammatical forms such as the tense forms, plural forms, possessive forms, forms for showing different degrees of comparison, etc.
2. ability to understand and use such features of structures as order of words, subordination, coordination of clauses, etc.
3. In addition to (i) and (ii), the ability to recognise grammatical errors and correct them and the ability to transform sentences from one type to another also fall under grammatical skills.

**Parts of Speech**

Words are divided into different kinds according to their use. These different kinds of words are called parts of speech. The parts of speech are: *(i)* noun; *(ii)* adjective; *(iii)* pronoun; *(iv)* verb; *(v)* adverb; *(vi)* preposition; *(vii)* conjunction; *(viii)* interjection.

*Noun:* A word used for naming any person or place or thing is called a noun e.g. Ashoka was a great king. *The rose* smells sweet. *His honesty* won him honour.

*Pronoun:* A word used instead of a noun is called pronoun. E.g. Ashoka was a great king and *he* lived like a saint. Rani is absent because *she* is ill.

*Adjective:* Adjective is a word which qualifies a noun. It tells us more about noun. e.g. He was a *brave* soldier. She is an *intelligent* girl. *Heard* melodies are sweet.

*Verb:* Verb is a word used to express an action or state. e.g. He *wrote* a letter. She *fought* bravely. He is honest.

*Adverb:* A word used to add something to the meaning of a verb is called adverb. e.g. He solved the problem *quickly*. He argued *logically*. She danced *gracefully*.

*Preposition:* A preposition is a word used with a noun or pronoun to show the relation. e.g. There is a cow *in* the meadow. The child is fond *of* sweets. A thing *of* beauty is a joy for ever.

*Conjunction:* Conjunction is a word used to join words, phrases, clauses and sentences.

e.g. Ram and Gobi are friends. He is poor *but* honest. *Though* he was poor, he was generous.

*Interjection:* An interjection is a word which expresses some sudden feeling.

e.g. *Hurrah!* We have won the match! (Hurrah expresses joy)

*Alas!* Our leader is dead! (alas expresses sorrow).

**Judgement Skills**

Judgement skills are also discourse skills, but they are of a higher order than those discussed under 'Discourse skills'. Judgement skills include style, register, organisation and relevance. They are so called because they involve choice of language that suits the purpose, which is a matter of judgement, when there are two grammatically correct sentences:

I gave Ram money to pay his fees;

I gave Ram so that he could pay his fees.

The second sentence is stylistically a neat sentence and it is therefore preferable to the first. We need to make such stylistic choices in our writing. Also, we should be careful not to mix the language of speech and the language of writing.

Such words as cop(policeman), brat (child), nosey (curious, inquisitive), that occur in speech/conversation should be avoided in writing. This is a matter of register, the choice of language that suits the written medium. Register is also a matter of choosing language that suits the subject. If your topic is one relating to law, you are justified in using words such as writs, plaintiff, defendant, ultravires, grounds (of appeal) etc. But in an article of general interest, the legal terms are best avoided. Thus, the use of the right register, the words that suit the medium of discourse (speech or writing) and the subject or field of discourse, (law, science, literature, etc.) is the second judgement skill. Thirdly, the choice of reorganisation of ideas or details in spatial, temporal manner or according to degrees of importance and finally the employment of relevant materials in writing form the two additional judgement skills.

**Discourse Skills**

A paragraph is not a list of unrelated sentences. It is a well knit unit where each sentence is linked to the others lexically, grammatically and logically. The lexical and grammatical links are referred to as cohesion and the logical link, coherence. *(i)* Lexical Cohesion; *(ii)* Grammatical cohesion; *(iii)* Coherence.

*Lexical cohesion:* Lexical (topical) cohesion is achieved by the use of synonyms and by repetition of key words.

*Grammatical Cohesion:* Grammatical cohesion is achieved mainly by use of pronominal forms.

*Logical cohesion or coherence:* Logical cohesion is achieved by linking the sentences employing logical devices which make paragraphs coherent.

## CHARACTERISTICS OF GOOD HANDWRITING

The following are the main characteristics of a good handwriting:

*(i)* Distinctiveness; *(ii)* Legibility; *(iii)* simplicity; *(iv)* beauty; *(v)* uniformity; *(vi)* spacing; *(vii)* capitalisation; *(viii)* punctuation; *(ix)* speed.

*Distinctiveness:* It means each letter should have a characteristic form of its own. It should be clearly and carefully written. The letters should not have resemblance with some other letters.

*Legibility:* Legibility of handwriting is of great importance. In order to ensure legibility in writing, the teacher should pay special attention to the five aspects of cursive writing i.e. letter formation, spacing, alignment, regularity of slant and quality of strokes.

*Simplicity:* The letters should be simple. There should be no unnecessary strokes in them.

*Uniformity:* Good handwriting is always uniform in style.

*Spacing:* The letters in a word, the words in a line and the lines on a page should not be crowded too closely together. Spacing is an essential feature of good handwriting. The letters in a word should be properly spaced. The words in a line should be placed at an appropriate distance from each other. A harmonious spacing of letters, words and lines is very necessary.

*Capitalisation:* Important words, proper names, and personal titles should be capitalised while writing. Capitalisation is of great importance. The first and last words of literary titles, the first word of quotation, etc, should be capitalised.

*Speed:* Good handwriting also requires a reasonable speed.

Having himself developed bad handwriting, Mahatma Gandhi lays emphasis on good handwriting in his basic education.

*Punctuation:* All punctuation marks should be used according to the meaning you want to convey.

**Punctuation**

Punctuation means the right use of putting in points or stops in writing. The following are the principal punctuation marks.

1. Full stop (.) [represents greatest pause and separation]
2. Comma (,) [represents shortest pause]

3. Semicolon (;) [represents a pause of greater importance]
4. Colon (:) [marks a still more complete pause]
5. Question mark (?) [ a greater pause after a direct question]
6. Exclamation mark (!) [ a greater pause after exclamation]
7. Dash ( - )
8. Parenthesis ( - -)
9. Inverted commas or Quotation marks (")
10. The hyphen (-)
11. The Apostrophe (')
12. The capital letter.

1. **Full Stop (.):**
   (1) Full stop is used to mark the end of a declarative or an imperative sentence.
   (2) It is used in abbreviations, but they are often omitted in modern style. U.S.A or USA M.L.A. or MLA

2. **The Comma (,):**
   (1) The comma is used to separate a series of words in the same construction
   India, Pakistan, Burma, Nepal, and Srilanka formed an Association
   (2) It is generally not placed before the word preceded by and. He was sincere and honest.

3. **The Semicolon(;):**
   (1) The semicolon is used to separate the clause of compound sentence, when they contain a comma. She was a noble, kind hearted lady; and we all respected her
   It is used to separate a series of loosely related clauses. Her court was pure; her life serene.

4. **The Colon (:):**
   (1) The colon is used to introduce a quotation. Bacon says:- "Reading makes a full man, writing an exact man, speaking a ready man".
   It is used before enumeration, examples etc. The principal parts of a verb in English are: the present tense, the past tense and the past participle.

5. **The Question Mark (?):** 1) It is used after a direct question. Have you completed your work?

   It is used after an indirect question. Tell me whether you know the truth.

6. **The exclamation Mark (!):** It is used after interjections and after phrases and sentences expressing sudden emotion or wish.

   Alas! Oh dear!

   What a piece of work is man!

   Long live the President!

7. **The Inverted Commas ("") :** Inverted commas are used to enclose the exact words of a speaker or a quotation

   He said, "I will meet you tomorrow".

   He said, "virtue is strength"

8. **The Dash ( - ):**

   (1) It is used to indicate an abrupt stop or change of thought.

   If my husband were alive – but why lament the past?

   (2) It is used to resume a scattered subject. Friends, brothers, relatives – all deserted him.

9. **The Hyphen (-):**

   (1) It is used to connect the parts of a compound word.

   Jack-of-all-trades, Passer-by

10. **Parentheses (—):**

    (1) Parentheses or double dashes are used to separate from the main parts of a sentence a phrase or a clause which does not grammatically belong to it.

    (2) A remarkable instance of this kind of courage – call it, if you please, resolute will – is given in the history of Babar.

11. **The Apostrophe (‘):**

    (1) It is used to show the omission of a letter or letters.

    Don't, e'er, I'd

    (2) It is used to form the plural of letters and figures.

    Dot your i's and cross you t's.

    Add two 6's and three 4's.

12. **The capital letter:**
    (1) It is used to begin a sentence
    (2) It is used to begin each fresh line of poetry.
    (3) It is used to begin all proper nouns and adjectives derived from them, Madras, Madarasi; India, Indian, Shakespeare, Shakespearean.

## CAUSES FOR BAD HANDWRITING

1. **Too much slant:** Its causes are (a) writing too near the body (b) thumb not mobile enough (c) point of nib too far from fingers (d) paper in the wrong position (e) stroke in the wrong direction
2. **Writing too straight:** It is because of (a) arms too far from the body (b) fingers too near the nib (c) incorrect position of paper.
3. **Imitation of bad examples:** Bad handwriting is sometimes due to imitation of bad examples.
4. **Use of ball pens, etc., from early stages:** Use of fountain pens or ball pens from the early stages is also responsible for bad handwriting.
5. **Lack of good sitting arrangements** is one of the causes of bad handwriting.
6. **Poor quality of paper and ink** is also the cause for bad handwriting.
7. **Improper posture:** Right and proper posture is necessary for neat handwriting-but bad postures can cause bad handwriting.
8. **Improper techniques of holding pens:** Techniques of holding pens affect one's handwriting.
9. **Running handwriting:** A large number of students do not have running handwriting. Pupils should be taught to write legibly at a fair speed. They should write neither too slowly nor too fast.

## DEVELOPING GOOD HANDWRITING

The following guidelines can be followed to develop good handwriting:

1. **Use of four line notebooks:** The use of four line notebooks will be extremely useful. If proper attention

is paid by the teacher to the size and spacing of letters, it results in good handwriting.

2. **Teacher's handwriting as a model:** The teacher's handwriting should be a model for the students. When he is writing on the blackboard, the students should be asked to watch the movements of his hands and fingers. The pupils should be made to understand the importance of proper strokes, uniform size and proper spacing.
3. **Individual attention:** The students' posture while writing should be attended to. They should sit comfortably in their seats in an erect position, with both feet resting on the ground and their bodies leaning slightly forward from the hips, but not touching the desk. Head should bend twelve inches away from the paper.
4. **Practice:** Adequate practice in writing should be given to the students.
5. **Charts:** Charts of good handwriting should be put up on the classroom walls. By constantly looking at them pupils will get their handwriting improved.

## TESTING WRITING SKILLS

There are many ways of testing writing skills. Objective type tests are not ideal to test the writing skill of the students. They are meant for testing the exactness of students understanding and knowledge. On the other hand, subjective type tests play a significant role in testing the writing skills of the students. We have to test the attainment of mechanical skill grammatical skill, judgement skill and discourse skill of the students in writing. How each type of subjective type test item can be used for testing the writing skills is explained below.

1. **Short answer questions**: These questions are very useful to test how far the learners are able to give precise answer.
2. **Long answer questions**: These questions are very useful to assess how far the students are able to organise the facts and present them in a logical sequence.
3. **Essay questions**: These essays are important to assess the critical and analytical thinking of the students. They are

useful to assess the judgement skill and discourse skill of the students. All types of essays i.e. argument essays, descriptive essays, critical essays and comparative essays help the teacher to test the various writing skills of the students. Their divergent thinking also can be tested.

4. **Precise writing**: This helps the teacher to test how far the students are able to condense the information and present the central theme in precise and accurate manner.
5. **Hints development**: This helps the teacher to test the imaginative and creative thinking and descriptive style of the students in writing.
6. **Letter writing (Personal)**: This will be very useful to assess how far the students are able to convey their feeling, emotion and affection in their writing.
7. **Letter writing (official)**: This is very essential to test how far they can communicate objectively in a matter of fact manner.
8. **Business letters**: These can be used to test how far the students are able to substantiate their view. Their ability to use the language successfully for business transaction can also be tested.
9. **Appreciation questions**: These can be used to test how far the students are critical in evaluating a work and how far they are ale to substantiate their view or argument with supporting evidence or detail.
10. **Summary writing**: This can be used for testing how far the students are able to analyse, organise and present the information in a cogent order.

*Note:* This is not an inclusive list. Only a few items which can be used to test the writing skills of the students have been discussed. There are more to be included. All the above items are very effective in testing the mechanical skill, grammatical skill, judgement skill and discourse skill of the students in writing.

## SUMMARY

Writing is expressing ideas, thoughts etc in words. Writing reinforces oral and reading works. Mechanics of writing refers to how a composition is arranged on paper. Spacing of words, paragraph alignments, spelling, punctuation etc are all parts of mechanics. The rules of mechanics are more like conventions. They are the trends followed by many people.

Writing is an effective way of communicating with others. It is a complex activity. It involves many sub skills which are unique and important in their own respects. The important subskills are visual perception skill, syntax skill, organising skill, grammatical skill, skill to write for content purpose and the skill to write relevantly.

Writing skills include various major skills. They are mechanical skill, grammatical skill, judgement skill and discourse skill. Mechanical skill includes planning stage, drafting stage and evaluating stage. Grammatical skill includes the ability to understand and use grammatical forms and the ability to recognise grammatical errors and correct them. Judgement skill includes style, register, organisation and relevance. Discourse skill includes lexical cohesion, grammatical cohesion and logical cohesion.

A good handwriting has great value. It appeals to the reader and makes reading easier, smoother and faster. The main characteristics of good handwriting are distinctiveness, legibility, beauty, uniformity, spacing, capitalisation, punctuation and speed. Having himself developed bad handwriting, Mahatma Gandhi lays emphasis on good handwriting in his basic education.

Bad handwriting makes reading very difficult and unpleasant. If affects understanding also. The common causes of bad handwriting are too much slant, writing too straight, imitation of bad examples, wrong use of pens, lack of good sitting arrangements, poor quality of paper and ink, improper posture, improper technique of holding pen, and lack of running handwriting.

It is the primary duty of the lower class teachers to develop good handwriting in students. In the beginning the use of four line notebooks will be extremely useful. Teacher should pay individual attention to students' posture, provide adequate practice in writing and use charts of good handwriting for the benefits of students. These measures will improve the handwriting of the students.

There are many ways of testing writing skills. Objective type tests are not ideal to test the writing skill of the students. They are meant for testing the exactness of students understanding and knowledge of facts and figures. Subjective type test items play a significant role in testing the writing skill of the students. Short answer questions, long answer questions, essay questions and composition exercises such as precise writing, hints development, letter writing, summary writing etc can be used to test the various writing skills of the students.

# Bibliography


Alless, and Campbell H.R. (1972) Teaching English as a Second Language Tata Mc Graw Hill, Bombay.

Arulselvi Evangelin (2009). Teaching of General English. Saratha Pathippagam.

Bright, J.A. (1982) Teaching English as a Second Language. ELBS Longman Group Ltd.

French, F.G. (1960). The Teaching of English Abroad 1, 11, 111 Oxford University Press, London.

French, F.G. (1966) Teaching English as an International Language. OUP, London.

Fries, C.C. (1955). Teaching and Learning English as a Foreign Language. University of Michigan Press.

Frishly, A.W. (1957). Teaching English. Longmans.

Geoffrey and Broughton et.al. (1978) Teaching English as a Foreign Language. (Routledge and Kegan Paul.

Gokak, U.K. (1965). Future of English in India (Asia, Bombay).

Gurrey, P (1966). Teaching English as a Foreign Language. Longmans Green and Co, London.

Menon and Patel, (1957). Teaching English as a Foreign Language. Acharya Book Depot, Baroda.

Nagaraj, Geetha (1996). English Language Teaching: Approaches, Methods and Techniques. Orient Langmans, Calcutta.

Rajeswari, N. (2009). General English. Shantha Publishers, Chennai – 14.

# Index

**Q**



**R**

❒ ❒ ❒ ❒ ❒ ❒